Between The Devil &
The Deep Blue Sea
Inch Chua

A Collaboration With
The Altar Collective

Between The Devil & The Deep Blue Sea
© 2014 Inch Chua & The Altar Collective

All rights reserved. This book or any portion thereof may not be reproduced or used in any manner whatsoever without the express written permission of both the copyright owner and the publisher of the book. Except for the use of brief quotations in a book review.

ISBN: 978-0-578-14571-6

First Printing, July 2014
001 of the Orchard Series.

Credits:
Cover design by Inch Chua
All artwork by Inch Chua

The Altar Collective
www.thealtarcollective.com

For Betty & You.

Ashes
taught me how to burn,
i've never been
quite the same anymo

Marks
taught me how to leave on
i've never been qui
the same anymo

Riches
taught me how to dro
i've never been quite the same anymo

```
Seems to me,
          no one stays the same anymore.
                    So let the concepts collide.
   i'm neither strong
              nor weak
       fufilled or empty.

                    i am only but stardust
                    we are only a speck

                    the earth is a starship
                              and we...
                         are voyaging.

       Water come put me in my place.
```

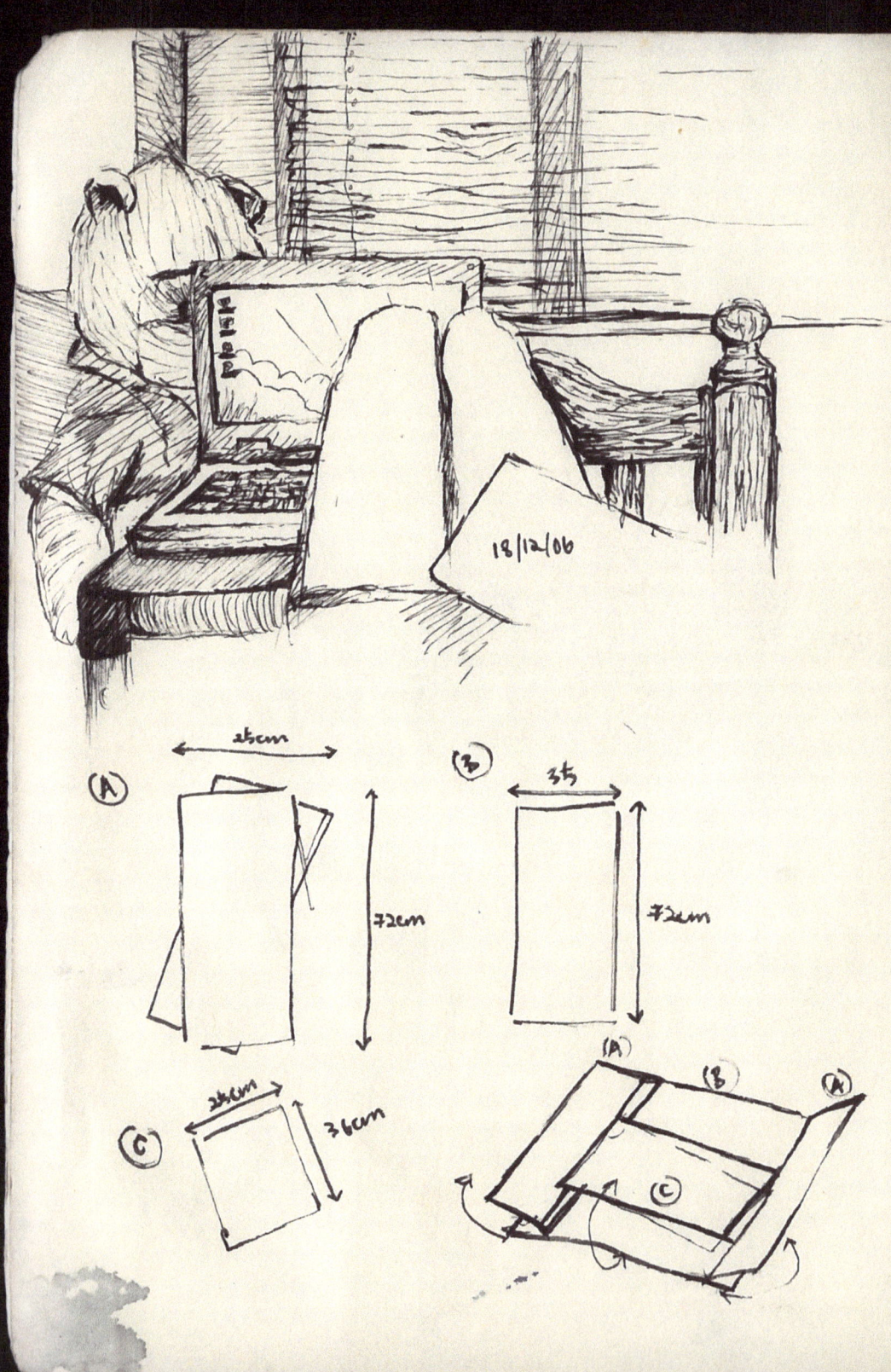

23rd Jan 2007

One thing I won't ever forgive ▬▬▬ for is the fact that he forced me to throw my diary away after reading it.

Guess, he just wasn't happy with what i wrote & what i truly felt.

These are some pages, i've managed to save.

Never forget. let this entry serve as a tombstone of the weak you.

RIP inch.

12 JAN 2007

I've wasted myself.... waste
At least I know I will never

i'm secondhand goods now.

chins up. happiness is a state of

Date: No.

)

se.

ALLURA

- Pheromones (3)
- Closure (3)
- New Say (5)
- Liberty (3)
- Diary Page (1)
- Ladeda (5)
- Limbo (4)

- Liberty (long intro)
- Pheromones
- New Say
- Closure
- Limbo (New intro)
- Ladeda

TSHIRT
Silk Screen Frame $6 × 1 = 6
Silk Screen INK $6 × 3 = 18
SQUEEZES $4 × 1 = 4
SS FILM $10 × 1 = 10
                            38

$2.50 = SHIRT
$500

```
       20              20          12 × 40 = 80
  25)500            × 2.50            +38
    80                 20            $118
    00               × 2.5
                      100
                      400
                     $500
```

ALLURA SET LIST

1. Rain
2. Sandwich
3. ~~damajazillion~~
4. Coldstarplayer
5. Loose Change
6. Limbo
7. damajazillion
8. ~~C0~~ Closure Redux

0. Limbo
1. Clandestine
2. Diary Page No. 13
3. Liberty With Wings
4. Coldstarplayer
5. Closure
6. Ladeda

ALLURA, MOSAIC MUSIC FESTIVAL 2007
PHOTO BY ALOYSIUS LIM

Allura Ideas

① icecream

gashpon

gashapon machines

vintage singapore

sparklers

vintage toys

Bomb bags

water guns

Taking its toll, visions a blur, to be heard.
Does everything, tempruments cold told.
Facing it slow, heard need to be bound, absent.
Does everything, your heart bounds, absent.
Does everything withers their presence.
Mindful that their own like the sun.
Pretending will be bursting like the sun.
My heart

Can you hear the whispering,
Chanting to the drowning sound.
Perpetually puncturing yet personifying
the visions around.
I can feel the distance, glaring from their eyes.
Is it natural, or my depravitive freedom to fly.

Feeling the void, my heart with a hole.
Do the words I say matter at all.
Taking it whole, my self esteem.
Does everything, my self esteem
Mindful

The water
then it
for you
undern
the let
yet un

M
yes

turning, churning faster than it should be,
...pe.
...ation, everything buried underneath my feet
...y feet.
...crumpled, new sheets are wrinkled. (oh)
...y clouds my rhythm.

...mething about you.
...re', something about you
...n your eyes,
...our eyes!

Lying naked in my bed, staring blank at the ceiling wall
wondering should I be moving on.
Taking chances over again, wondering should I take
this leap of faith. Should I be moving on.
...n the devil and limbo lies a hard place.
...a hard place.
...tes tail me and I'm falling head over heels
...er heels over you.
The letters are crumpled, newsheets are wrinkled.
Yet an uncertainty clouds my rhythm.
Between the devil
and limbo.
Between the devil
and limbo.
Yes, no, maybe so, I don't know.

Clandestine

...ence is absent.
...bursting like the sun.

This is a story about a boy I know
with the heart and sweetest soul.
This is another tale to tell about
the love I solely own.
Everyplace at his deep breath.

Plans all fall, as the seasons
change time. But words we port
are enough for the ones we are.
I just need to tell you
three simple words.

With fragile hands,
you love me over and over ag...
no again.
For everyone turns
to that in our bottom me.
This is the second part
about the words you have to tel...
This is another corny love
letter for my womano
who sits and waits by my
window.

Plans all fall, as the seasons
change time and wond...
We spent a lot of enough
for the ones we are.
I just need to tell you...
three simple words.

CHICKEN STUFF

1 Sliced Apples
4oz chopped mushrooms
100g ?

1 5 cloves onion & garlic
some Rosemary, thyme, sage
some ?

salt & pepper to taste.

- milk
- butter
- salt, pepper } mash potatoes.
- lamb or beef (minced/diced)
- carrots · oyster sauce
- mushrooms (shitake, brown, white,
- Asparagus/broccoli, button, portobello.) } filling
- onions
- garlic puree · sesame oil.
- olive oil

1. Boil potatoes, with a pinch of salt + vegetable stock
2. Prepare beef by seasoning it with olive oil + sesame oil, sugar + oyster sauce + salt + pepper. Let it marinate at least 2 hours.
3. Meanwhile, prepare carrots + asparagus. Slice, chop and boil them with potatoes.
4. Mash potatoes add a tablespoon by a tablespoon of milk while you mash. Fork drain and let aside.
5. Add salt + pepper + butter. And microwave till fluffy, then set aside.
6. Sautee mushrooms with onions and garlic + olive oil. When water is drained out with non Add minced vegs. Meatmix. Stirring till done + garlic.
7. Lastly add the veggies with a tinge of herbs.
8. Find heatproof bowl or a square-shaped baking ware. (assorted herbs) place the meat on the bakeware, make sure the layer is filled.
9. Lastly place the mashed potatoes on the top.
10. Season with, herbs, salt, pepper and a few knobs of butter. Put in oven for 30 mins on low heat: 120°C.

Stuffed saddle of lamb.

1. Take water out of mushrooms with pan + olive oil, drain mushrooms.
2. Olive oil, butt spinach. Add with mushrooms.
3. Add cream cheese into the spinach + mushroom mixture + nutmeg.
4. Add an egg yolk. Then into the fridge.
5. Season lamb with salt, pepper + sage (+ rosemary) + garlic.
6. Place stuffing in center of the saddle. Wrap and tie with kitchen twine.
7. Marinate 4:30 min or overnight at least.
8. Roast on pan, with garlic, sage and olive oil.
9. When it starts to brown, add butter.
10. Then baste into the oven. Roast for an hour or so.

Beef chocolate + cinnamon

Ingredients:
- beef meat (chuc): 3 pounds → 1 kg
- sherry wine
- beef broth
- 1 onion
- 2 cloves of garlic
- bitter-sweet chocolate
- thyme
- 1 tbsp flour
- cinnamon
- bay leaves
- black pepper + salt

★ youtube.com/watch?v=NxFTY8k5SE

Method:
- Caramelize beef with butter + vege oil.
- Take beef out.
- Sweat onions with garlic → salt + pepper
- DON'T OVERCOOK GARLIC
- Add flour → Add sherry.
- Simmer → Add beef.
- Add beef broth.
- Add thyme, bay leaves.
- Bring it up to a simmer
- Then set timer for ONE HOUR & A HALF
- Simmer under low heat.
- After all the timer goes off, add chocolate.
- Put lid back on. Go on for 30 mins.
- Let it cool off, put in fridge overnight.
- Scoop fat off.
- Then heat and cook the sauce on Med-low heat.
- Serve beef.

Buttermilk fried chicken.
- Marinate: salt + pepper, paprika, buttermilk.
- Breading: eggs + buttermilk.
- Add mustard + a bit of Japanese salt + pepper.
- Pantry breading: cake flour + salt + pepper.
- 4 hr min or overnight.
- Dip chicken to breading mix. (Fry chicken + big oil.)

Coq au vin w/ apples / chicken thighs w/ apples & onions

Ingredients:
- chicken thighs
- onion
- apples
- 1 glass dry white wine
- butter + olive oil
- 1 lemon
- chicken stock
- mustard w/ flour
- salt + pepper

- Olive oil → on pan → chicken thighs + onion + apples
- Wait → simmer → wine + butter
- Mix flour → simmer with dijon mustard
- Salt + pepper → lemon juice
- simmer + serve

Chocolate brownies
- 2 eggs
- 1 cup sugar
- ½ stick of butter
- 1 block chocolate
- ½ cup plain flour
- (cookie ingredients)

1. MUSHROOMS
2. SPINACH
3. NUTMEG

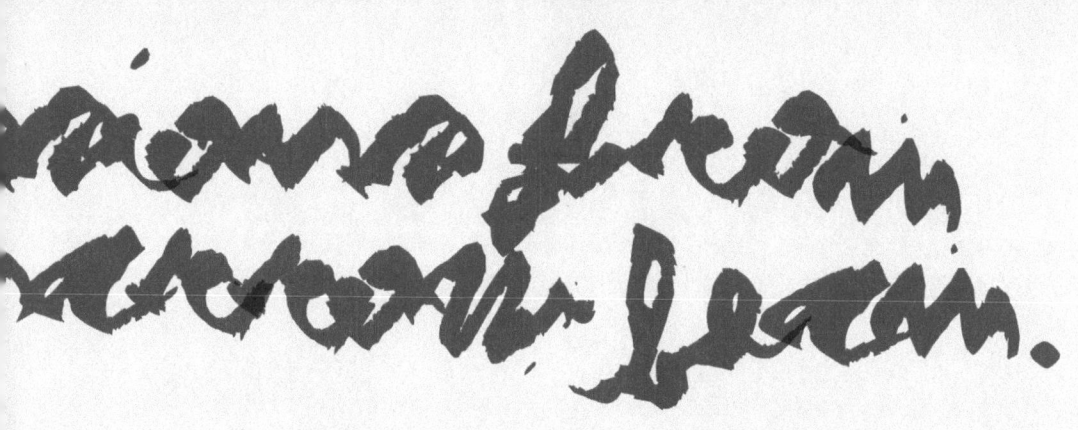

feel you trickling in my veins
poetically paraphrased into sequences of sonnets.
Unpredictably captivated,
feeling out wit and out matched.
I breathed you in.

Still
there you were.
Standing motionless,
illuminating the constellations
tempting me to touch fire.

Holding on tight to the thoughts
triggered by your minute gestures
Without second guess i second guess myself.

Are you aware i need you?
Are you even aware?

our questionably queer responses
continues to
undermine my sober senses.

Are you aware i love you?
Are you even aware?

Dancing my way along narrow beams,
you're the only reason that's keeping me dry.
I am but violent colours
meeting your gentle gestures

You held my hand
and winked twice.

You looked at the skies
with your head tilted back.
While i watched you
and the reflection of the universe
existing in the the gleam of your eyes.

Tempted to touch fire.

21/03/2007

Have you ever felt life literally
slipping away from you fingers?
its not right. its just fucked up.

that kitten was barely even walking
with misty blue eyes.
...it fought so hard to live.
why couldn't you have done anything!?

you just sat there,
while the warmth melts through
the cracks of your cupping hands.

you can't even help a sick kitten!?
inch, you're such a useless dumb shit.

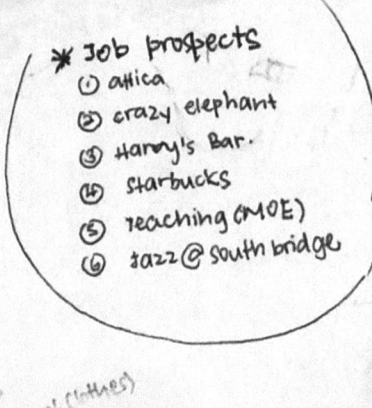

* Job prospects
  1. attica
  2. crazy elephant
  3. Harry's Bar.
  4. Starbucks
  5. teaching (MOE)
  6. jazz @ south bridge

(1) 60 × 4 = 240
    80 × 1 = 80
           320

(2) 320 × 3 = 960 bucks
    60 × 3 = 180
    80 × 3 = 240
           420

    420 × 3 = 1260 bucks

(3) 420 × 4 = 1680

25 MARCH 2007

```
  Mount Pleasant Animal Hospital
32 Whitley Road Singapore 297824  PH:6250-8333
```

TAX RECEIPT (OPEN)   *** # 57119
NVOICE GST NUMBER M2-0039191-8
hua Yun Juan (13625)   for   Echo

	Cat Crem w/~~o~~ Ashes	52.50
	:	
	Total to be taxed	50.00
	GST content	2.50
/07 12:24 pm	**TOTAL TO PAY**	52.50
by		

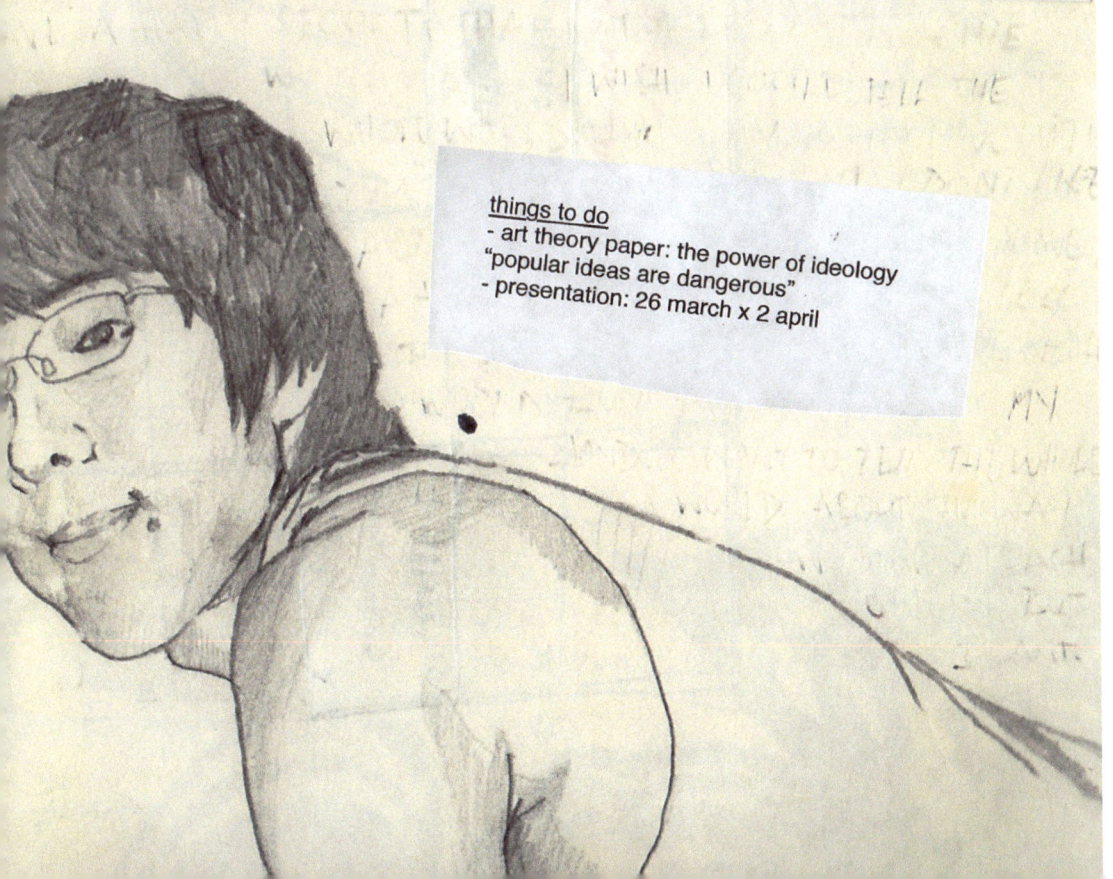

things to do
- art theory paper: the power of ideology "popular ideas are dangerous"
- presentation: 26 march x 2 april

controlled chaos

01 Aug 2007

RANT FOR SILENTLY UNCONTENT

verse 1

~~The weeks have been damming past me and I've completely lost track of the time~~, dates, my emotions, thoughts and ~~house keys~~.
Somehow in the sudden constant of the moment, although it may not seem quite fair, I'd still like to blame everything that happened on you.

× | You're one of the world's greatest enigma

Stop making me ponder-er   ~~Prechorus~~   cause you
Stop making me wallow-oh   Abusive behaviour   are a
Stop making me ponder-er   you're damn enigma   effing
Stop making me wallow-oh   # you say you don't know, oh   enigma
                                             and you're spacing out out out

Chorus

My organs are in your hands   my lungs are drenched
and your putting it all over the place   *cause I've given up with this debate*
swinging inside outside, # your playing games   sweet wrappe-
~~do I look like a playground to you~~   I FEEL THE ACHE IN YOUR HEAD
~~turning it down left right~~   ↙ CONVIENTLY DISPOSABLE
~~do I look like a joy ride to you~~.   quit phyinds games.

Now listen well, cause I'm trying to tell you that
you melt me down into this ~~insignificant~~ mindfully stupid
~~batsty~~ desperate idiot.

Quite frankly by now, I've established pretty well that
you leave me cluelessly uncontent half the time.
And its almost impossible how it MH could get through your thick skull

03 Aug 2007 - ~~Silently Discontent~~ / Sangwich

Somewhere in the sudden constant of the motion,
Although it may not seem fair
I'd blame it all on you, blame it on you.

stop making me ponder-er
stop making me wallow-ow
stop making me ponder-er
stop making me wallow-ow

And you are known as an enigma
Yes, you are known to me as an enigma

Its in your hands,
and you put it all over the place.
Swinging inside out, you're breaking it
You're a <u>damn disgrace</u>.
Take it right back, and giving it back
and you <u>put it all over the place</u>.
Turning inside out.
This is for the silently discontent.

(pre-chorus + chorus.)

Start to wonder where i am
and where i'm <u>go</u>ing to.
where i'm going to.

You say you don't know,
you say you're spacing out out out
You say you don't know,
you say you're spacing out out out
You say you don't know,
you say you're spacing out out out
You say you don't know,
you say you're spacing out out out
You say you don't know,
you say you're spacing out ~~out out~~

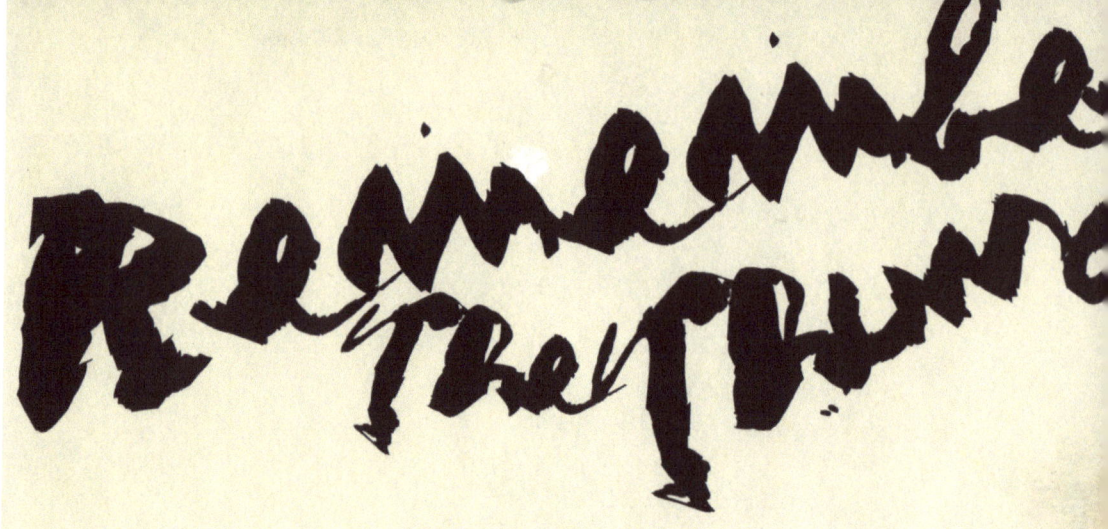

It just hit me.

I am never going to see you again.
I am never going to talk to you again.
Never going to laugh with you again.
Never getting to share my stories with you anymore.
Never going to hear your stories anymore.

Never.
Its such a harsh word.

Wayne, i'll be sure to look for you when its my turn.
You still owe me a paddle pop.

[CAPO 3RD FRET]

VERSE
```
x x 2 1 2 x  ⎫
x 2 1 2 x x  ⎪
x 3 2 x x x  ⎬ x4
2 x x 2 x 2  ⎪
2 x x 2 x x  ⎭
```

PRE-CHORUS
```
1 x 1 x 1 x  ⎫
x x x x x x  ⎬ x2
x x 2 x 2 x  ⎭
```

CHORUS
```
x 2 4 4 3 2  ⎫
x x 2 2 2 x  ⎪
x x x 2 3 2  ⎪
3 ———        ⎬ x3
2 ———        ⎪
x 2 2 x x x  ⎪
x x 2 2 2 x  ⎭
```

Ah ah ah ow.

Pins & Needles

It seems that simple things don't make out to be simple at all
its stupid why I'd always find myself like a fly on the wall
pins & needles, ah ah ah ow.

And now, I'm drowning by the dryness of my patience and I,
decay like rusted thoughts you breath away.

I trusted in the moment
you'll take and you'll choose.
Yet you chose another somehow you choose,
a different way and now I'm left,
jaded by the things that you do.
Hey you are, the way you said you would be.

It seems that stupid things will always be stupid after all
its funny how I'd find myself facing the wall
pins & needles, ah ah ah ow.

Tuesday, June 3, 2008 — Purity leads to Intimacy

I came back home today with an evident smile mixed on my face. I actually leaned against my closed door and sighed like a prissy pansy. It's been a while since I felt this innocent content & comfort in my heart.

I love wasting my time away with him. Last night, while I was listening to his voice, I could feel the yearning, the loving & the calling of a hurt person. It got me reflecting on what a pathetic sport I am.

I loved all of them. All them ex-lovers with all my thinking heart. Gave all that I could give. Yet none wish to reciprocate. I'd countlessly pick them over me. Perpetually swallowing my pride; allowing the compromise to slowly eat me away.

Its doable, but not sustainable.

Why didn't any of them looked at me with endearment? Why was I always so shrouded with fear? The fear of abandonment to be specific.

Maybe it's the gambler in me. You know, giving myself away for something worthwhile or at least proportionate to my biddings in return.

<u>Stupid lords. Purity leads to intimacy.</u>
I wish I understood it earlier.

gambler's remorse can be such as nip in the butt. All the past few years of failed emotional investments just felt like such a waste.

Anyways, it was nice enough for him to check up on me. I honestly feel better now. It's ~~just~~ been a while since someone saved me from myself.

discern. "

~~Too many~~

Too many time I've fell in love.
Too many times the lessons never learnt.
Too many times I've given it away
~~I just But~~ I wouldn't have it any other way.
I guess my heart just sways this way.

I will forever find myself
Coming out of a rut
Leaving nothing but the high frequency's
and a sound .... of my
   heartbeat

and one yet to discern   Yet not enough to discern
Too many times ~~the people have turned~~
Too many times I've got my finger burnt ~~x~~
Too many times, yet I still can't discern. I've given it away
~~does my head even function the right way~~
~~I should be an expert but I'm still a Jame~~
would I really have it any other way
I guess my heart's just meant to break

Too many times,
I've fell in love.
Too many times,
The lesson's never learnt.
Too many times,
I've given it away
But I wouldn't have it any other way
I guess my heart's just sways this way.

Too many times,
I've got my fingers burnt.
Too many times,
Yet it's so hard to discern.
Too many times,
I've given it away.
But I wouldn't have it any other way.
I guess my heart's just built this way.

And I,
Will forever find myself climbing out of the rut
Hearing nothing but the high frequencies
And the sound of my... heartbeat.

Too many times
Oh too many times
I couldn't even see signs when I cross the line
Wouldn't eat, wouldn't sleep, wouldn't even give a damn
But I wouldn't have it any other way
I guess my heart's just meant to break.

```
x 7 x x 7 x  ⎫
x 7 x 7 7 x  ⎬ verse
x x 5 5 5 x  ⎭

x 3 2 x x x
x x x x x x
x x 5 5 5 x

x x x 3 x
x 3 2 x 3 x
x 3 2 3 3 x
x 1 x x 3 x   ⎫
x x 2 x 2 x   ⎬ CHORUS
x x 3 x 3 x   ⎪
x x 5 x 5 x   ⎪
x x x 2 1 1  ⎭

3 x x x x x   ⎫
x x x x 1 x   ⎬
x 2 x x 3 x  ⎭
1 x 1 x 1 x

5 x 5 5 5 x  ⎫
6 x 6 6 6 x  ⎬ bridge
7 x 7 7 7 x  ⎭
```

Sunday, June 27, 2008

Love is best seen as devotion & actions not, an emotion.

"Dear Children, ~~#~~ let us not love with words or ~~to~~ tongue but with actions & in truth"
— John 3:18

What seemed like just another glorious day of sightseeing today turned into a full blown existential education. Thank you, Gaudi.

Reality never felt this realllll. It's as if this particular freeze frame in time was waiting for my arrival, so that my bungled life could un-glitch itself.

I'm <u>never</u> going to be the same again & that thought brings me this strange feeling in my stomach.

It's unnerving that i feel so much confidence in something i can't explain. It's probably cause I'm not articulate or intelligent enough to conjure a tangible & logical explanation to justify this experience. But i'll get there. The skeptic in me, won't leave quietly tho.

Cold ✱ pcym

The wind blows
& else knows.
Soon we'll start bending
on as the story goes
we'll wake up unremembered

Singing
la la la la.

So turn off the lights & say goodnight yourself

I was crawling & walking backwards
like a dog searching for a rainbow.
But I am an empty vessel pure to pretense & intent
Hopefully not at someone's else expense.

On plates they throw
the anthem blows but I'd say
"Bring on the spotlights"
oh, the cycle goes
we'll be glowing to fade.

Thursday, July 3, 2008

I want to go back in time right now & relive my last week in singapore before I left.
Somehow, I've this feeling its going to be different when I get back.

Thursday, July 10, 2008

Hello, meet Inch Chua. Your very own emotional punching bag!

Friday, July 17, 2008

Youthful, love & lust.

Deep thought thinking time: Flee the evil desires of youth, & pursue righteousness, faith, love & peace, along with those who call on the lord out of a pure heart.

— 2 Timothy 2:22

The puzzle fixed's wrong,
                                    for years
        been
    I've stuck in lost roads of truth,
    the silence's ~~it~~ a siren of tears

    ~~try~~ Our timing's always wrong
        the pain's~~is~~ been here for ~~far~~ too long.

    I'm losing words to talk
    The emptiness starts to talk
                                        got
    and breaking down's the option I ~~see~~

    see I'm of no luck at all

    I'm not so cut out for love
    no one's arm I ~~can belong~~
    cause no one ever gonna find me
        the signs are clear that

neverending attention

tell her you love me, the back and haunt her, turn in circles. cunny back as nearer. not so you said it was baby. wade to the forest. But me. No or sh [unread] to herd.

IN CHAGRIN CORNERS WE WILL MEET,
WITH WARMTH TO SHARE. WE'll TAINT THE SHEETS
IN YOUR HANDS, MY HEART YOU'LL KEEP.

The puzzle fixed is wrong
but i'll just keep playing along
losing's not hard at all
It's the emptiness that kill me,
that no one's gonna fix me.

I'm losing words to talk   that stalks.
The silence's a siren   here for too long
The pain's been   the only option I see
And breaking down's   all.
See I'm of no luck at   for love.
I'm just not so cut out   ever belong
No one's arms I could   no one's gonna
The signs are clear that
           Find Me.

The current's getting far too strong
I can hold on but for not too long
On repeat I'll play your song
And maybe try to convince myself that no one's
gonna Save Me.

I'm sorry I mistook you for the one
who's gonna save me.

Saturday, August 30, 2008

The lonely heart always greets the sun.

Today's been a long somewhat erratic day. My emotions feel shaken, stirred & served to an undeserving aristocrat. (whatever that means).

Maybe's my period or maybe its the crazy emotion confrontation I've been experiencing! Okay. I know I was being sarcastic there but to be honest, I really don't know what's wrong with me. I just can't seem to get a grip of my feelings today.

Did a show at the Singapore Zoo today — it was interesting. I really like the whole concept & idea of the show but the turn out was horrible. Much credit for that goes to the rain & the fact that the zoo is in freaking Mandai. It didn't seem like they could have broken even or raise the money they needed for their cause. I'll be praying for the organizers.

Then I headed to Baybeats to catch YAWA. I reckon they did a great job, evidently nervous but awesome nonetheless. I'm so proud of beni! ♥

All of which I spent most of the day, one on one with Low Han Quan. It was nice, honestly. Long talks in the car, laughing & joking. It reminded me why I fell in love with him in the first place. He's really a nice simple guy.

Through out everything tho, mark was the only thing on my mind. Its been a strange day of radio silence from him. All I could think about was how much I miss mark, why he wasn't around, why hasn't he checked up on me or asked about the shows.

"I'm with hq now... where's mark?"
Apparently no where near and is no way concerned today.

I'm a little too old to be feeling lonely. but i do. I felt lonely pretty much for the whole day even though I was perpetually surrounded by people. I feel alone while I'm sitting at my desk writing this & I still have the loneliest hour to face before I fall asleep.

oh no. the sun's coming up.

Sunday, August 31, 2008
I Reckon.

I reckon I'm not one of his priorities.
oh well inch, get over it.

Things just don't seem normal...
...anymore.

Tuesday, September 2, 2008

Mummy made me breakfast today.
german breakfast minus the meat.

are you wondering how that works?
I'm still on it too.

La Sagrada Familia.

Tuesday, Sept 9, 2008

Clarity Clinches Control

a chance is a chance. an explanation is an explanation. a second chance is a second chance. & an asshole is an asshole - period.

why the hell do you always buy every excuse from everybody? why the hell do you always compromise with yourself.

you're foolish you know.

for pete sake, mean it when you say its the last time. on another note.... who the hell is pete?

Friday, Sept 12, 2008

Youthful love & lust

"Flee the evil desires of youth & pursue righteousness, faith, love & peace, along with those who call on the Lord out of a pure heart."

— 2 Timothy 2:22

DATE 21-09-08
TIME 4pm to 6pm
VENUE

you are invited
to join us for the baptism of
inch chua

LIGHT SNACKS WILL BE SERVED

<u>Saturday, Sept 20, 2008</u>
A circumcision of the heart.

inch.
these are your last few hours.
Afterwich, <u>you will die</u>.

"Therefore, as God's chosen people, holy & dearly loved, clothe yourselves with compassion, kindness, humility, gentleness & patience. Bear with each other & forgive whatever grievances you may have against one another. Forgive as the Lord forgave you. And over all these virtues put on love, which binds them all together in perfect unity."

— Colossians 3:12-14

diving into the deep

The storm is a swirl.
emotions a stir & i'm taking cover.
Pacing around back and forth
walking around,
× finding the sounds of ~~hidden in the ether~~.
× footprints that lead to truth.

× from beyond
× secrets of the world
× great enigma
× restless deep
× infinite

The pavements ~~ahead~~ abound, no end to be found/
I'm pacing slowly, moving along with right kind of wrongs. & little shaky feet.

| 5 7 7 4 5 5 |
| 5 7 5 7 5 5 |
↓

× 4 3 4 × 4
× 2 × 2 3 ×
× 2 1 2 × 2
(double time)

verse

haven. is
the ~~trumpets~~ are calling.
Inviting pleasant happy thoughts

⟨ A death to the Heart
  a circumcision for the heart ⟩

ideas

Into the deep blue sea.
~~drowning~~ submerged / under water / aqueous oblivion.
neck deep / dancing on the surface.
walking on water / swimming in my head /
basking? / floating / aqueous heaven

(divin into)
aqueous oblivion.

x 57675 /6 x2
x 46654

x 24432 /6 x2
x 46654
→ hang.

bridge

x 57675
x 57765
x 46654
2 x 272 x

x 57675
x 57765
x 46654
x 24432

Chorus.

the spark is stark
making its (mark)

I'm no longer heavy
      ↓
she so heavyyyyyy~~~!

floating around,
   feeling astral.
              ↓
        spiritually aroused?
feeling aroused spiritually?

what is life about?
Embracing the wonders of everything!
Seeing the magic in normality!
Chasing dreams/visions → clouds? } clues of
      - footprints!   the universe.

Aqueous Oblivion

The storm's a swirl
Emotions a stir and
I'm taking cover.
　　　Walking around,
Finding the sounds to my selfless keep.

　　　　The pavement's abound
　　　No end to be found and
　　　I'm cruising slowly.
　　　　　Moving along,
With right kind of wrongs
and little shaky feet.

　My sheets are calling, i͏
　A death to the start,

　　　　　　(D͏
　Aqueous oblivion
　Aqueous oblivio͏
　　　　　He's swi͏n

Maybe i'll wake up light and learn
　　　　　　I know i've sti͏
As long as i know ͏

The spark is leaving me stark
Making its mark
and i'm no longer heavy.
Floating around,
Feeling astound with the normality.

I've figured it out,
What life is about and
I'm feeling holy
Running about,
chasing clouds and footprints now.

pleasant happy thoughts.
mcision of my heart.

to)
t in hazy vision,
t in the divine,
 my mind.

be concur that the fire does burn.
a long long way
sit still and obey.

If you and I both rule the world
~~we'll be seeking high, far & low~~
imagine you & me in a hole we dug.

X7687X
X767X7
5X7675
X7687X

Hey babe, someday you & I will save
the world. It will be just you
and me ~~and~~ the super tag team

digging holes.
I treasure love
 ‾‾‾‾‾‾‾‾‾‾
 noun   verb.

Hey babe, someday you & I will rule the world
and it will be you and me and no more
animosity to ~~star~~ bare. riches of the world,
we will share.

5X665X
4X44XX
5X665X
4X44UX
9X999X

pure
=gold.   beating up bad guys,.
          keeping our eye on the prize.

577 65X
799877
9X999X
4X444X

Nothing never last ~~forever~~,
but i ~~want~~ to make this last
~~till~~ we turn to prunes.

pull the trigger

Nothing ever really lasts,.
but i hope that it all won't pass
till we're prunily? old.

ing Youth
15 Minutes present

9837 MILES TO TEXAS.

BENEFIT SHOW FOR INCH CHUA.

aturing acoustic sets by Talk To The Walls, Plainsunset,
racal, B-Quartet, Amateur Takes Control, A Vacant Affair
d Inch Chua.

erchandise available for sale.

nue: 15 Minutes @ Lasalle College Of The Arts
me: 8pm
ate: 5th February, 2010 (Friday)

Sunday, Oct 12, 2008
Closer.

Sorry. Its probably the word you hear the most from me. & for that I'm sorry too. I wish it could be something else that glorifies you.

but nooooo.
You keep hearing sorry after sorry after sorry. I don't want to be a let down, I don't ~~don't~~ want to turn my back on you. & I most definitely don't want to ever walk away willingly from you like it never meant anything.

But it feels as if I'm incorrigible, I just don't seem to get things right.

I'm really sorry, Lord.

"You will seek me & find me when you seek me with all of your heart"

& that all I can do.

Conscience.

I let the beast in and
Its taking taking me well into control
Walking heavy on shards of glass
There will be no end until i say no.
But its dauntingly haunting me now ow ow.

I said,
I let the beast in and
Its breaking breaking promises
Walking heavy on shards of glass
There will be no end until i go.

Pardon me now,
While i rendered my conscience unconscious.
Starve yourself, for a little while.
But it will linger (on)
linger (on)
deliriously on your finger
like a splinter with a motive in mind.
Who gives.
i'm just not cut out to be a saint.

(handwritten notes:)

...iously
...onscious
about
thy conscious conscience.

i let the beast in,
i let the wolf in,
i let the devil in.

who gives,
i'm not cut
out to be
a saint.

Sunday, December 7, 2008

The Devil

" They say the safest road to hell is a gradual one - the gentle slope, soft underfoot, without sudden turnings, without milestones, without signposts."

- C. S. Lewis, Screwtape Letters

The concept of duality, specifically the duality of men, intrigues me. It's fascinating how the human state of being has a habitual pattern to exist in two folds... where the nature of these two qualities usually greatly differs. Two opposing forces, dependent of either existence.

mind and matter,
circumstance and choice,
light and darkness,
needs and wants,
peace and war,
dividedness and unity.
and today's subject of rumination...

good and evil.

Reading *Screwtape Letters* has really gotten my wheels turning. It just dawned on me that evil isn't exactly what i've made it out to be. I'm baffled i've never spent a thought about it before.

Discourse about goodness has always had its fair amount of airtime at the dining table. While curiously, the subject of evil remains taboo in most social settings. It's not even a topic one would even consider thinking about when they're alone. I mean, i've always felt nervous thinking about having to think about it.

Understandably, of course. But it just loomed on me that denying the existence of evil or avoiding the understanding of it is probably just as dangerous as having an obsession with it. And, in fact, "evil" is probably most successful at getting to you when it is subtle or non-existent in one's eyes.

"Nothing is very strong: strong enough to steal away a man's best years not in sweet sins but in a dreary flickering of the mind over it knows not what and knows not why, in the gratification of curiosities so feeble that the man is only half aware of them, in drumming of fingers and kicking of

eels, in whistling tunes that he does not like, or in the long, dim labyrinth of reveries that have not
en lust or ambition to give them a relish, but which, once chance association has started them,
e creature is took weak and fuddled to shake off."

— C.S. Lewis, *The Screwtape Letters*

Note to self: Be conscious of how much rumination would be too much.

So traditionally and mythologically, evil is personified in the form of the devil. He/She/It is presumed to be the source of evil, opposing all things good and commonly regarded as the archrival to the omnipotent, omniscient and omnipresent God. If this is true, it would mean that God and the Devil are at war for the ownership of my soul. I'm really not sure how i exactly feel about that. It doesn't seem right that i'm such an innocent bystander while my mortality is being gambled away like that.

Ever since i was a kid, i would feel this nagging dark energy... as if evil was lurking in me. It sounds dramatic but its only because the definition of "evil" is socially dramatized.

From what i've witnessed and know, the root of all evil stems from self-centredness. If so, the entity responsible for evil... this darkness... isn't a horned red man with a pitchfork, but... he/she/it exists as a mirror. A mirror that shows a reflection of the self. A mirror that magnifies whatever that sits across it. Which naturally directs one's attention to one's various flaws, personifying the insecurities and impeding one's view... quite literally from anything around them. Its isolation of the self to the self. And the voice i so constantly hear is my own that leaves me suspended in disbelief in order to make sense of what i see in front of me. It's truly my own doing that i fall into the rabbit hole of measuring my self worth to a reflection of me.

I am my own devil.

My falter into a crisis of faith, is the result of staring too long at the mirror. Its easy for a mirror to use truths to lie and its easy to believe when its me persuading myself.

I should be looking beyond the mirror, and focusing on others.

SET ONE

TOXIC — INCH ON GUITAR & VOCALS

CLANDESTINE — INCH – GUITAR & VOCALS / MARK – ELECTRIC GUITAR

AQUEOUS OBLIVION

FIND FIX & SAVE

SAMPLE TRACKS USED // INCH – GUITAR & VOX // MARK – ELECTRIC + BACKUP

PINS & NEEDLES

INCH – GUITAR & VOCALS // MARK – ELECTRIC GUITAR + BACK UP

TOP OF THE WORLD

INCH – VOX // MARK – GUITAR (ACOUSTIC)

DEVOTION IN REALITY

RETURN OF E FATCAT

SAMPLE TRACKS USED // INCH – NINTENDO DS & VOX

RULE THE WORLD

20.12.08 - CONVERSATION WITH BANANA(S)ELVES.

B1: INCH CHUA, YOU ARE A SAD DELUDED SOUL.
HOW COULD YOU HAVE THOUGHT FOR ONE SECOND
THAT GOD HAS FORSAKEN YOU?

B2: I AM AN EMPTY VESSEL; VULNERABLE, LOST AND INCOMPLETE.
I SEEK TRUTH BUT WHICH VERSION OF IT IS ABSOLUTE?
I ALWAYS JUST WONDER, " HOW ARE WE SUPPOSE TO KNOW?"

B1: THROUGH JESUS.
HE DIED FOR YOU, SO THAT YOU CAN BE FORGIVEN.

B2: I KNOW THE STORY.
BUT IS JESUS REAL? DID ALL OF THAT REALLY HAPPENED?
I MEAN IS THE BIBLE EVEN REALLY THE WORD OF GOD?
HOW DIFFERENT ARE THESE STORIES AND PARABLES
TO OTHER COLLECTIONS OF STORIES THROUGH TIME
LIKE GRIMM'S FAIRYTALES? AESOPS? HARRY POTTER?
IT WAS AFTER ALL WRITTEN BY HUMANS.
YES, YES YES, I UNDERSTAND ITS WRITTEN BY PEOPLE
UNDER THE INFLUENCE OF THE HOLY SPIRIT.
HOW DO WE KNOW <u>FOR SURE</u>?

B1: ALL SPECULATION BUT THERE'S NOTHING TO PROVE THAT
ITS NOT PLAUSIBLE. SO ITS A MATTER OF CHOICE.
IT ALL BOILS DOWN TO CHOICE, INCH.
A CHOICE TO EXERCISE FAITH.

B2: WHAT ARE MY OPTIONS?

B1: TO LOVE GOD WITH ALL YOU'RE HEART AND BELIEVE THAT
THE TRUTH IS WHAT THE BIBLE MAKES IT OUT TO BE.
OR DENYING ALL THAT HAS HAPPENED IN THE PAST FEW MONTHS.
HAVE YOU NOT SEEN THE HAND OF GOD IN YOUR LIFE?

B2: IM NOT ENTIRELY SURE.
I GET THE FEELING HE DOESN'T CARE ABOUT ME
TOO MUCH SOMETIMES - I MEAN WHY WOULD HE?
THERE ARE PLENTY OF OTHER PEOPLE IN THE WORLD DYING,

CRYING AND HURTING.
I JUST HAS MY STUPID FIRST WORLD PROBLEMS.
WHY WOULD HE NEED TO CARE ABOUT ME?
I DON'T NEED IT EITHER, AND I THINK HE KNOWS IT.
WOULD BE NICE IF HE SHOWS UP FOR THEM.

B1: DO YOU TRULY BELIEVE YOU DONT NEED HELP?

B2: EVERYONE NEEDS SAVING.

B1: GOD HAS BLESSED YOU WITH THE PEOPLE AROUND YOU.

B2: SO WHAT IF I DONT HAVE THAT KIND OF FAITH?

B1: BEING SKEPTICAL IS HEALTHY.
TRUTH STRENGTHENS WHEN IT IS QUESTIONED.

B2: I JUST WISH GOD WAS MORE TANGIBLE

B1: SHALL WE PLAY A GAME?_

I can feel the pins & needles of the games
until
this life will fiddle,

I've played the pawn, the knight & bishop,
rolled the dice & moved my pieces,
spent more time on my knees,

All seems clear.
And hi
I've got to get over myself.

to gain some rationality

I've played the pawn, the knight & bishop
rolled the dice and moved my pieces
spent more time down on my knees,
waiting for a sign or signal.
But it was no cause I can't read you

I've traveled to Kermit, seen the hope that's left turns
Sailed the clouds, just for a while, came back down.
reviewed the options
And once again, I'm ballast & stuff

~~Majestic~~ Fangirl love

(m - mute)

```
X7687X        The
X767X7        ~~with~~ ~~the~~ glittered lights,
              they flickering from the reflection of
5X7657                 your eyes
X76m5m        they glow like
```

```
5X665X
4X444X    →   3X333X
              2X222X
```

The lithium mirror fogged up
and I'm watching get shaving

~~XXX~~   CGCEGC ~~tuning~~
      XX323X
      XX545X
      XX43X4   ff

He greeted me with smile and apologized
for he cold only stay for a while.
It breaks my heart a little but it assures me
that he wouldn't leave me (behind)

Devotion In Reality.

He greeted me with a smile
And apologized for he could only stay for a while.
It breaks my heart, but he assures me.
He won't leave me behind,
oh not behind.

He cheated me with lies,
And realized that slowly tearing me apart
He took the time to repair me
Not leaving me behind,
oh not behind.

oh not behind.

i cannot ask for better friends. thank you. ♥

(handwritten draft, partially legible:)

little melting pot of mine. my ~~all I've got~~ lights up ~~the~~ glow~~ing~~ a spark of ~~R~~
~~the colours all of the world all neatly aligned.~~
to
~~my~~ comes ~~to greet and~~ greets the skyline. cherry ~~birthday~~
~~and my heart is in my hands~~ and my heart's pure ~~ready~~
as the colours of ~~light~~
is this red dot of mine.

~~people all are~~
the colors of the city
the people all around me. ~~comfort~~
~~I install "they're place"~~
the sounds ...

it's connected
4 million
I couldn'...

oh oh o...

thi...

Red Dot V.4

I couldn't settle down somehow
And find myself a tree to hide.
Its not like its easy but
i'll find my way to park my pride.

Could it be the nature of the city?
the foreign inferiority
the dying urge to be accepted as a somebody?
Disconnected to the nation
Four million population
I couldn't even hide, how i feel

[
Whoa oh oh
Whoa oh oh
I wouldn't trade my stay
Whoa oh oh
Whoa oh oh
But it would be nice to see some change
]

This little red dot of mine,
maybe small in many eyes.
But i really don't mind

Could it be the nature of the city?
the people all around me
the superficial things we all place in priority
Disconnected to the nation
Four million population
i couldn't even hide how i feel

The World & me.

"we are all in the gutter but some of us are looking at the stars." — Oscar Wilde.

I've always felt like I was neck deep in a hole I dug for myself. "gutter" might be too strong of a word for this hole. It's more of a trench.

In geology, trenches are created as a result of erosion by rivers or by geological movement of tectonic plates.
In civil engineering, trenches are created to install underground infrastructure or utilities of provision & communication.
In the military context, trenches are dug for defense purposes.
In archaelogy, the "trench method" is used for researching & excavating ancient ruins.

Destination trench awaits everyone.

Some might have arrived via an erosion of circumstances. Or... driven by the intent of establishing an emotional infrastructure. While others burrow to excavate the past of introspectionism.

Mr. Wilde was right: we do live underground. But with most respect, I rebuke it being a gutter.

Passion is not public performance, but personal holiness.

Sunday, Nov 29, 2009
Prayer for fat cat.

i cannot be more proud of matt yap!

i know he's going through some serious changes in his life right now. I cannot be more happy for him that he has the desire in his heart to... for the lack of a better ~~or~~ phrase... "be a man" & walk towards your direction.

Lord, I pray you send your angels to watch over him & perpetually prompt him when he's confronted with difficult situations.

please don't stop reminding him that everyone around him loves him & most importantly, that you love him. please lift his burdens of "letting anyone down". He needs to know he's not alone in this, Lord.

Return Of the fat cat

destiny calls
do you feel the fire burning like it was
It's the weight of the world, hidden behind the cause
It's the weight of the world, is your heart heavy, ready to bawl?

Cold as ice, you face the early parade.
does the purple light know your name?
I know the feelings you'd find seems hard to change.
Just in two years time, you'll break away.

destiny calls.
do you see the beacons beaming across the shore?
Is the weight of the world, egging you more along.
Is the weight of the world, is your head heavy,
ready to bawl!

(chorus)

your shoulders will crack
they will burn under the sun
but I won't ever let it get to your head.

TUNING — C G C E G C (open C)

[CHORUS]

```
2XX12X
9XX89X
XX X7X7X7
```

[PRE-CHORUS]

```
5XX5XX
7XX7XX  (5 count)
7XX89X
7XX7XX
```

[VERSE]

```
X5XXXX
X7XXXX
X9XXXX
7XXXXX
5XXXXX
```

Please kiss me one se ophi.
A room with a vacant chairs

do you
have third
thought your own
you were
dead?

bridge _____

```
XX5 45X
4X434X
8X878X
(12)(12)X(10)(10)X
7X7X7X
```

i grew up with a lion in the house,
                         and the only way he knew
                        how to show that he loved me
                                      was to hunt.

                he was..
         proud as a lion should be,
         fierce as a lion should be,
      aggressive as a lion should be.

i unfortunately feared him more than i loved him.

           his power came from unpredictability and his
absolutes. i remember thinking to myself, that he was
undeserving of his kingship. that, his majesty was an
           illusion created in my mind by pre-existing
 formalities, his general disinterest in everything,
                   and his unapproachable demeanor.

somedays, he'd prowl about the house, sneering at
every little tiny thing. one moment he'd be licking
his paws. the next pinning me down with a roar of
intimidation. somedays, he'd sleep all day.
somedays, he'd leave and not be back for weeks,
months.

       until one day, he left and didn't come back.

            the distance between us was no longer merely
 figurative. his disinterest became abandonment. The
              unapproachable became out of reach.
years past, and i... forgot what it was like living
with a lion. but i never forgot what it was like to
be fed as fresh kill was left on our doorsteps each
month.

i grew up with a lion in the house,
                         and the only way he knew
                        how to show that he loved me
                                      was to hunt.

i unfortunately love him and fear he'll never know.

I HAVE A FACE & SO DO YOU.

When I was 10, i was mauled by a dog and ended up in hospital with 135 stitches on the face and 2 stitches on my right palm.

i don't remember much.

But i do remember the look on my mum's face when she found me: confused and writhing in our bloody wading pool of a porch with the flesh falling off of my face.

i then
felt arms,
saw air,
tasted blood,
smelt old car leather,
and heard the engine trying.

i don't remember much.

But i do remember the look on the nurse's face when they saw my condition : losing colour as they unreasonably wasted a copious supply of bandages.

i felt bandages,
saw bandage.
tasted bandages
smelt bandage
and heard the winding spools of bandages harmonizing with the electrocardiograph monitor.

i don't remember much.

But i do remember the look on people's faces when they see saw me : purple and bruised with pieces of thread sticking out of every corner of my mangled face.

i have a face, and so do you.

And with every new face thats introduced to mine, it has become a personal sport of mine to observe people's reactions.

facial muscle twitches, nervous grins. misplacing manners with stares fixated at my scars. lips would move almost independently with cordial small talk. A personal favourite thus far, is the non-blinking charitable eye to eye stare, where they refuse to acknowledge the presence of the scars, feeding their brains an instruction manual that commands every fibre of their body to not stare.

New or old... i don't forget faces.
i mean, how could I
when most of them won't let me forget mine?

wallflower

Hello world, i'm a mismatched glove on the shelf of a hardware store.
Its not like I know how i got here from before.
time just took me on its tide.
Hello world, i'm part of the world but i don't qualify to be, part of society's soci—
'Cause i will always cruising on my own.

Hello world, do i

I wish that someone would notice me,
its not like I'm so hard to see.

look like the girls in the magazines,
owned and photoshopped to the last degree, oh spare me would you please.
I wish that someone would wanna know me.
it's not like I'm so hard to see.

I'll just hide in my garden, plant my own trees and watch me grow.
But no no no, they won't let me be.
As they stand still and tease.

Hello world, is it weird that i fit in your colony?
I was always just known as the black sheep of the family.
Cause I was always never walking on the dotted line.

I just hide in my garden, plant my own seeds & watch me grow.
it won't be much longer,
till i become a pretty wallflower.

Cold, Conned & Conquered

Pieces of you,
ourselves we lose.
We're falling.

People we knew,
finding excuses to be amused.

Breathe in slowly,
take a step outside.

(breathe)

Laid out like an open book,
you're broken broken.
Wasted is the good on you.

You're cold, conned, conquered.

"Fame is vapour
and only earthy certainty is oblivion"

Blame the accuse,
ourselves we choose.
We're falling

Fame we pursue,
finding excuses to be amused.

Breathe in slowly,
take a step outside.

Cold, Cold is the sheep with no wool.
Back, Black is the shade of my skin.
I could stay on the third degree, b
ut my heart's on wholesale.
Yes, my hearts on wholesale.

Someday,
we'd be having laughs over some cakes and tea.
You'd ask, how has love been for me
and i'd reply cordially.
Then you'll, notice the blush on my face.
We'd smile, soaking it all until the bubble burst.

Dark, dark is the lane off the road.
Black, Black is the shade of my skin.
I could stay on the third degree,
but my heart's on wholesale.
Yes, my hearts on wholesale.

Someday,
we'd be having laughs over some cakes and tea.
You'd ask, how has love been for me
and i'd reply cordially.
Then you'll, notice the blush on my face.
We'd smile, soaking it all until the bubble burst.

Cold, cold is the sheep with no wool.
Black, black is the shade of my skin.
Plain, plain is the simple we seek.
Fake, fake is the lie we all use.

Cold, cold is the sheep with no wool.
Black, black is the shade of my skin.
Plain, plain is the simple we use.
Fake, fake is the lie we all seek.

"love without sacrifice is like theft".
— Nassim Taleb.

hurt.

Cold, cold is the sheep with no wool.
Black, black is the shade of my skin.
plain, plain is the simple we seek.

```
 X7577X        I could stay on the 3rd degree
 X544XX        cause my heart's on wholesale!
 ─────                           on the
 XX665X ⎫     you could be ~~my~~ first degree
{X544XX } XL  ~~hope~~ your heart will hold me.
{X546X7 ⎭      but
```

SOMEDAY, WE'D BE SHARING LAUGHS OVER SOME
CAKES & TEA. YOU'D ASK HOW HAS LOVE BEEN FOR ME &
I'LL REPLY CORDIALLY. THEN YOU'D... NOTICE THE BLUSH
ON MY FACE. WE'D SMILE — SOAKING IT ALL.

```
7 X777X    [X5455X]  BREATHING IT ALL.
X7677X      [hang]  — BELIEVING IT ALL.
XX665X   ↑          UNTIL THE BUBBLE BURSTS.
```

dark, dark is the lane of the word.
Black is the shade of my skin.
Fake, fake is the lie we all use.

Have it your way,
It's your will over mine.
Have it your way,
It's your will over mine.
~~It's not like the grand scheme of things,~~

It's not like ~~it means a thing,~~ it ~~means~~ could all means thing,
against, the grand scheme of things.
      you &
It's all just a wait~~ing~~ for ~~our next~~ my
~~to the wait,~~ ~~if the~~ next pending option.
~~so I'll~~
~~He my wait for~~ but i'll fake, till the
          trust
You could say I've fallen from grace,
but ~~it wasn't like~~
     ~~I ever~~ even there in the first place?
           was I
~~oh I'm just all turned~~
~~I guess I better hurry~~

~~guess~~ I'll turn myself inside out
So ~~you can~~ just take it all.

Have It Your Way

Have it your way,
its your will over mine.
Have it your way,
its your will over mine.

so just take it all,
and turn me inside out.
just don't leave me in the dark.

Have it your way,
its your will over mine.
Have it your way,
its your will over mine.

its not like it could all mean a thing
against you and the grand scheme of things
so i'll just wait, for the next pending option.
you could say i've fallen from grace,
but was i even there in the first place.
so you could just take it, take it all.

so just take it all,
and turn me inside out.
just don't leave me in the dark.

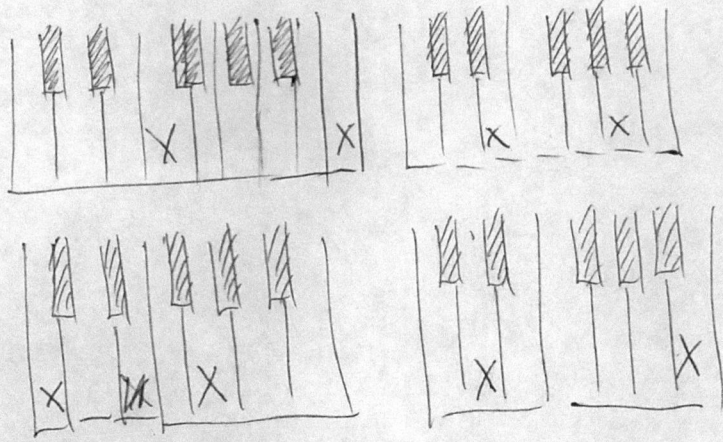

Dear Warhol, dream diary

Andy Warhol is dead.
              and i killed him.

      I was on trial for the crime, but yet
      i've no recollection of what happened

                Nothing.

         If i did or if i didn't. I just...
              blacked out. Memento style.

No one believed me - Not Mark, not Rhord.
   Not anyone except a guy named, Dany.

                 Sweet nice guy i recalled.
    Someone i don't recognize from real life.

However much to my suprise,
     before i was sent to the gallows.
         Dany spoke to me,
     confessing that HE was Andy Warhol.

He faked his death and framed me for it
    so that he can live a normal life.

            He apologized, quite genuinely
       and said: "Thank you for understanding

                          ...you always
                             do"

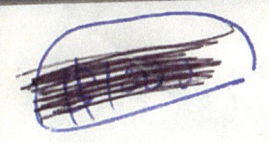

the nubs of the universe
went out for some coffee & tea.
It seems like they won't return
till the candles are blown & a year redeemed
thou people will pass, like parcels in the mail regimen

nothin

~~the~~ the smokeshit ceiling.
everyone's gone home
and you've got nothing but a bellyful of bake batter.
To make you feel more alone.

You should know know know know
the joker's not on you.
Stop collecting bottles of yourself
cause you deserve much more room on your shelves
I won't won't won't find no one like you
don't need to send in the clowns today
Cause you know I'll be the one won't forget your birthday

bridge
x 3 2 x 3 x
x 3 1 3 3 x   x 2
x 2 x 2 3 x
5 x 5 5 5 x
x 5 4 5 3 x

the candles are lit
the candles blown
another year
another vision

happy sad
𝍲 III IIII
 III

wednesday, december 22, 2010

Hello old journal, its been awhile... its my birthday today. feeling pretty good actually. 2010 has been pretty kind to me. my favourite year thus far. definitely one for the books with many milestones made.. Hoorah.

Had a quiet celebration with mummy today. i figured it would be a good ~~day~~ day to tell mum about richard's offer and my plans to leave home. it's strange cause... many years ago, i wouldn't even bother asking mum. not to say i wasn't nervous she'd say no this time, cause nah.. clearly telling her about my intentions to leave her on my birthday was a mere coincidence. No strategic planning involved at all. Yup, thats my story and i'm stickin to it. Either way, deep down i knew she was ready to say yes. which she did, along with the expected amount of cautionary advice.

Letting go has been a huge thing for mum is it weird that i'm actually feeling pretty proud of her that she's so willing?

e never fails to surprise me. its kind of
refreshing to see your parent... learning & and
changing and making the effort to push
themselves out of their comfort zone.

its not easy for mummy, but she's letting me.
part of me is actually excited that she'll be
missing me. okay, that sounds mean. let me
rephrase... its nice to be in a position where
I'm missed by mummy. its like our absence
works as a reminder that we love each
other. something like that.

Also, mummy told me she loves me today. :)

like
~~The~~ string puppets ~~more in~~ it sways in anyway,
~~As long the~~
Anyway was the wind as long as there's money to be made.

it's not a matter judgement,
~~but of fiscal pay~~ or fiscal aid.
It's a matter of the retribution as a civil slave.

You're a sad sad, sad situation.

It's a pain i'
It's a bloody pain
for me to be crippled wasted below &
still walking with broken bones.

like ~~the~~ white collars it's assumed, unstained
lying to themselves that
~~Pretending that~~
~~But~~ reality ~~won't~~ reflects the same.

taste it
remark

anomaly

It's a matter of principle as a civil slave

I'm not your
Systematic automatic machinery.
cause I'm "♩♩♩♩♩♩seabird" it seem ♫ ga

CIVIL SHAME

LIKE STRING PUPPETS,
THEY SWAY IN ANYWAY.
AGREEING WITH THE WIND.
AS LONG AS THERE'S MONEY TO BE MADE.

IT'S NOT A MATTER OF JUDGEMENT
OR FISCAL AID, ITS A MATTER OF RETRIBUTION AS A CIVIL SLAVE.

YOU'RE A SAD, SAD, SAD, SAD SITUATION.

{ IT'S A PAIN
IT'S A BLOODY PAIN
FOR ME TO BE CRIPPLED WAIST BELOW
& STILL WALKING WITH BROKEN BONES.
IT'S A SHAME
IT'S A BLOODY SHAME
FOR YOU TO TURN YOUR BACK ON ME
CAUSE YOU COULD HAVE BEEN THE ~~MELODY~~ REMEDY.

LIKE WHITE COLLARS IT ASSUMES UNSTAINED
LYING TO THEMSELVES THAT
REALITY REFLECTS THE SAME

A CIVIL SLAVE

```
X7X7XX        X4XX5X
5XX5XX        X3XX5X
X5X7X                       #2X2I2X
X4XX5X                      4X45XX
X5XX7X        6X455X        ~~X4465X~~
X7XX3X        X5455X        X434X4
              32X2XX        ~~X435X~~
              X2X23X        X2I.2X2
              X7X7X
```

Eye's closed
i feel the fire burning.
Burn bright
The warmth it all surrounds me

It burns because you love me.

Burn bright for me baby,
i could see, i could see you glowing.
Burn bright for me baby,
i could see, i could see you glowing.

Eye's closed
i feel the fire burning.
Burn bright the warmth it all surrounds me

Hands clasped.
i feel my heartbeat racing.

Stand down, cause i might burst in tears.

It burns because you love me.

Burn bright for me baby,
i could see, i could see you glowing.
Burn bright for me baby,
i could see, i could see you glowing.

See you glow
See you glow
See you glow
See you glow.

Exodus

Stay

- mark john
- family
- friends
- thunder rock
- comfort
- save $$$
- break the system
- risky chance
- How? visa? How?

Leave

- youth smiles upon you
- new experiences
- new challenges
- achieve beyond asia
- education

Thursday, July 28, 2011

The people asking me to stay better be people who go to local gigs and watch local musicians.

i might have invited the crosshairs but it is a little ridiculous to flail your bitterness and insecurities on me.

maybe i'll look back and roll my eyes at the shit i've said. but for now, if what you say isn't remotely constructive — i will roll my eyeballs out at you.

on another note... YOU CALL THAT JOURNALISM!?

Friday, October 17, 2011

Love constrains us. People say it like it's a bad thing. "Constrain" is a strong verb but quite frankly misunderstood. The word's present dictionary definition has suffered the social ill-fate of negative connotations attached to it. Other words that suffer from such similar circumstance include "conservative" (an adjective, not to mistaken for the right-winger of a noun) or the word "awful" (which I use to mean "awe commanding" before sarcasm was invented.)

> **con·strain** [kuh n-streyn]
> **verb**
> 1. to <u>force</u>, compel, or oblige: *Love has constrained her to stay in Singapore.*
> 2. to <u>confine forcibly</u>, as by bonds.
> 3. to <u>repress</u> or <u>restrain</u>: *Singapore's cultural landscape constrains the her creative growth.*
>
> **Word origin:**
> 1275-1325; Middle English *constrei* (*g*) *nen*
> < Anglo-French, Middle French *constrei* (*g*) *n-* (stem of *constreindre*)
> < Latin *constringere*
> < Latin *con-* / *stringere*
> *con-* (a prefix meaning "together" "completely")
> *stringere* (to bind, tie, draw tight)

So in some sense, one only feels compelled, obliged, confined forcibly because love's constraints completes us. We become <u>responsible</u> for <u>taming</u> love, drawing it close and mixing it in our own dna. The repression one feels stems from the depravity of completeness.

Packing my life up in boxes has truly commanded a lot of emotional practicing from me. With each suitcase I fill, it's assurance that bit by bit, I'm vacating — tearing the tissues of my completeness. And no matter how hard I pack every little speck in every cranny, I am going to

Friday, October 14, 2011

leave something behind. forever doomed to walk this earth in a state of constraint; missing something or someone or someplace while the constraints of a love tug away at me from across continents.

I should take comfort that i know where to find said missing elements, but i guess i'm just ranting because,

(1) being in transit is the loneliest of hours.

(2) being in the lagrange point of my two lives is causing me to orbit around in vacuum with my existential angst.

love constrains | love liberates.

They say truth is always somewhere in the middle, right? So maybe...

(1) love's constraints liberates?
(2) love's liberty constrains? The freedom of love constrains?
(3) liberty loves constraints? no. liberation loves constraints.
(4) constraints liberate love ~~or constraint~~

Food for thought.
on another note, language is awesome.
or should i say, awful.
old ~~so~~ school awful.

You're a little old   (shame on you)
                              shame on you)
to be chasing young skirts like you did before.
~~I crossed the line when I got a little~~ anxious
Don't be flirting with ~~me~~
                                  Public
If you can't ~~test in front~~ of the jury (shame on you
           in the presence.   shame on you)

Your ~~~~ was once
Youth ~~is~~ ~~maybe~~ a gift, ~~but it's your wisdom you should~~
                              ~~this live passed its date~~
                              ~~but its passed~~

  like if   One turd that should have
  would do   translated into wisdom
  like it   like it should have.
  would be
      ~~it~~   one a
        Your youth may ~~do~~ a gift, but it failed
                  ~~but it's lost its translation~~ to be
                       ~~its wisdom~~   translated into
                           ~~to~~   wisdom

        Just maybe in another
        universe were age is not a number.

      ~~But~~ ~~its sorry that~~ gravity is calls for the 1st
                          ~~against you~~
                      ~~will fall~~ kill your curiosity.

      I'm you sorry you curiously

x5463x
x8786x
x2x25x

You're the artful dodger, 3x333x
the mystery joker,
~~I can't read your mind~~, x2x23x
You're hiding behind
your wall of humor. x5455x
85543

You're the artful dodger,
~~the my~~ ~~heart beat stopper~~. the gut
~~prelude~~
I can't figure you out,
or get a little closer. [fold]

How could I have jumped
into the cold with the unpredictable.
the rest is predictable
How could I have jumped
into bed with the ~~dangerous~~ ticklers.
~~it's too futile~~. why did I have so
challenged
unseen

You're the artful dodger
~~my heartbeat stopper~~ the comic actor
I'm afraid of my wit

Adventures with Eehohohoh

London

13/11/11 — 5/12/11.
Benita Lim, Evelyn Choo, Melissa Poon & me.

Liverp[ool]

This is the first re[al?] ~~tece~~ where you ~ travel. I feel k[inda] drove mos[t]

- × Stoke-on-trent
- × Staffordshire
- × church visit
- × open mic
- × James & Mel.
- × campus adventure.
- × cooking cookout!

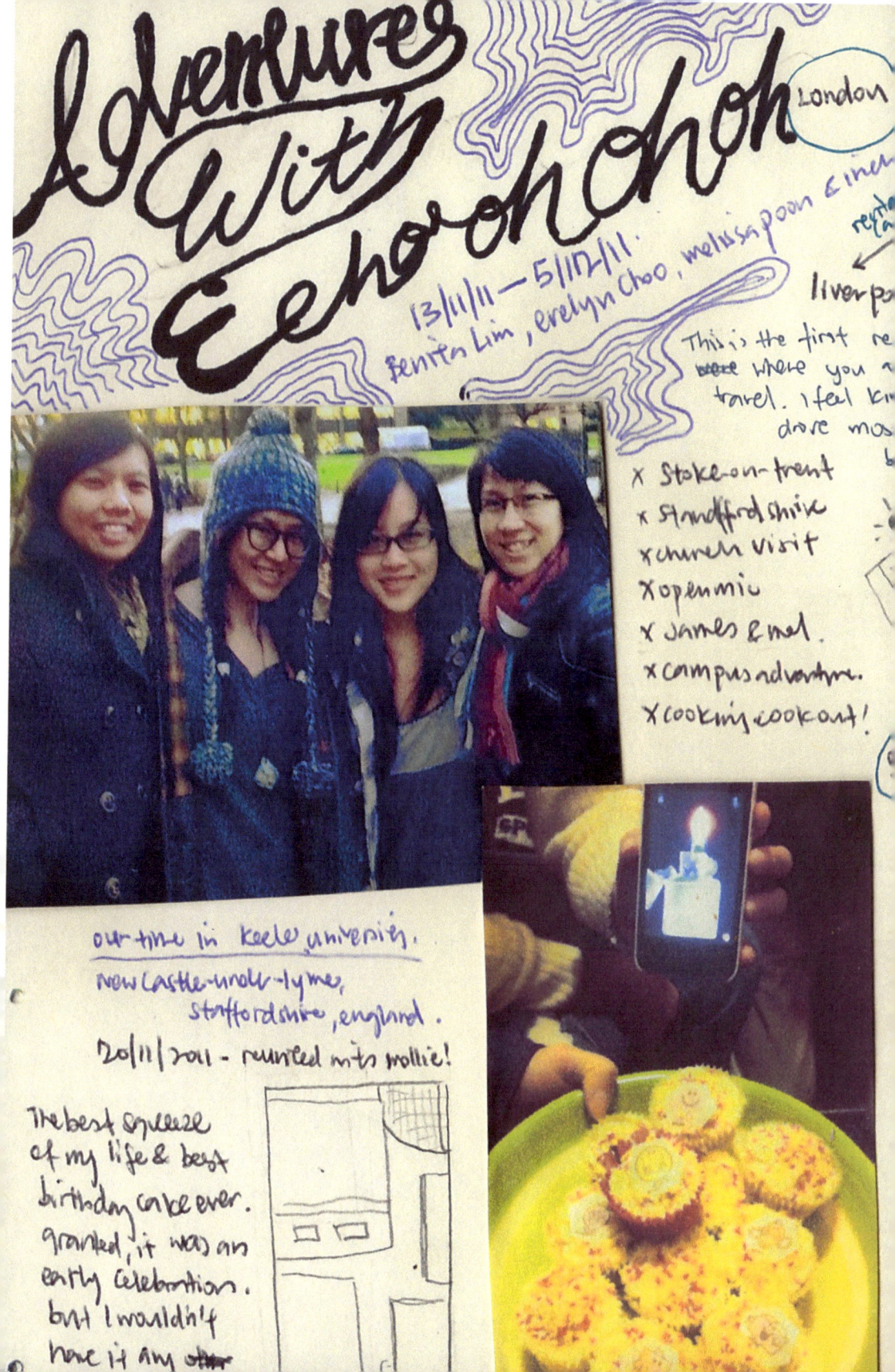

our time in keele university.
newcastle-under-lyme,
Staffordshire, england.
20/11/2011 - reunited with mollie!

The best squeeze of my life & best birthday cake ever. granted, it was an early celebration. but I wouldn't have it any oth[er]

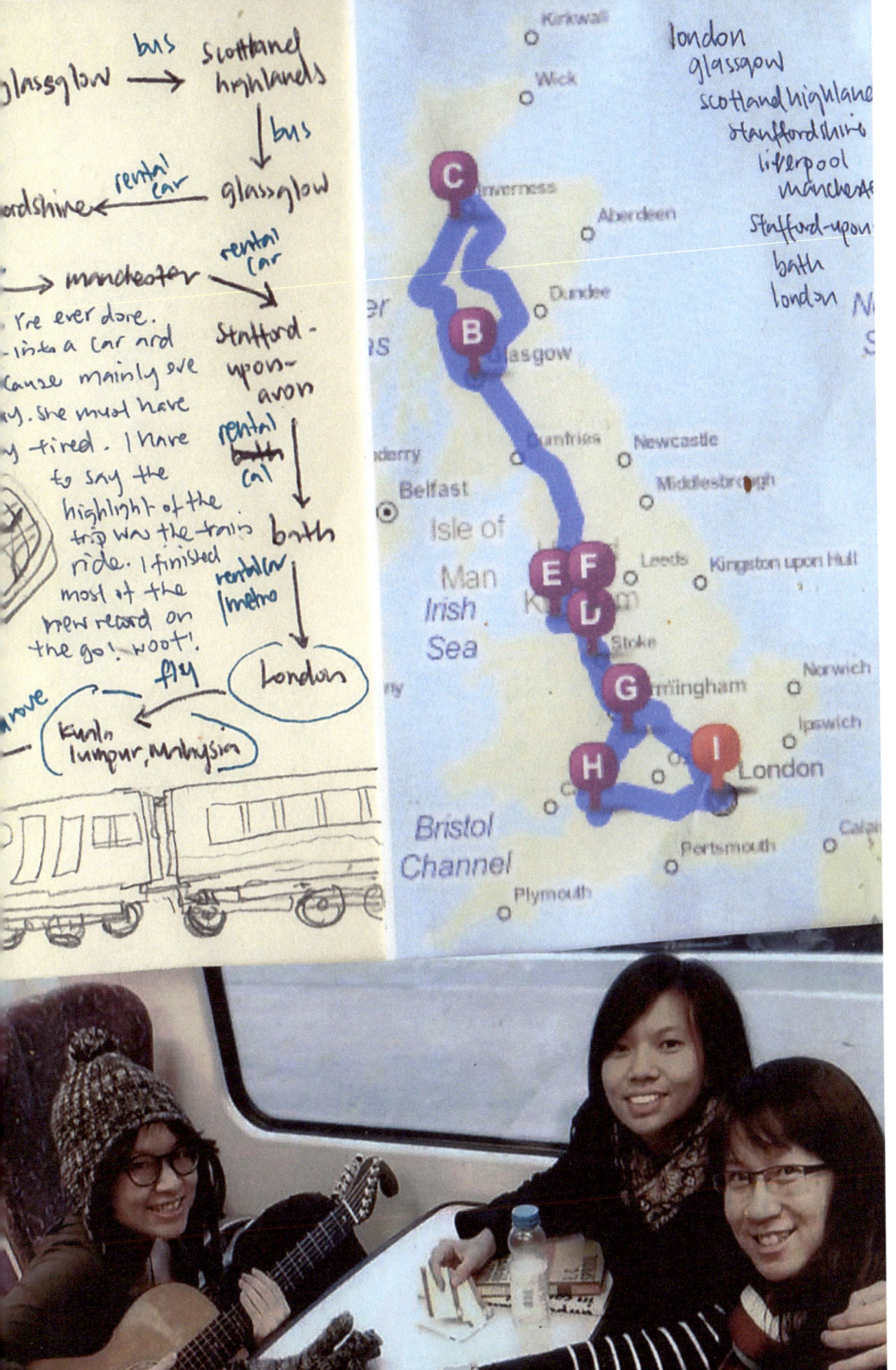

THOUGH SHE BE BUT LITTLE SHE IS FIERCE

A MIDSUMMER NIGHT'S DREAM

dear michielur,
beni and i gave you this notepad right after you told us you had been been confirmed to play for the Canadian music fest. and we are so happy for yooooo!! may this rind of sheets, though plain and small, equip you in your quest to conquer the world. love ya little girl. :)

in His love,
~~evelyn~~ ♡
CHOOBS
23 November 2011

Reminder: initial excitement.

dear michielur,
beni and i gave you this notepad right after you told us you had been been confirmed to play for the Canadian music fest. and we are so happy for yooooo!! may this rind of sheets, though plain and small, equip you in your quest to conquer the world. love ya little girl. :)

in His love,
~~evelyn~~ ♡
CHOOBS
23 November 2011

x57xxx   who am i to give advise
x87xxx   when i'm a guilty
57xxxx   sin spender spender-er
x6½xxx   what am i to be but unwise
         when I've got my hands up
         surrender surrender.
x13xxx   (Ouu. Gaudi. How did you
x32xxx   get so good good good..
x54xxx
         who am i to resist
         when i'm logger a beast of burden
         what am i to be but reminded
         when I know the answer is
         bitter better.

         (OOuu GAUDI)
         tell me your secrets, your
         tales of chivalry, love & misery

         show me your
         daggers.
         yours tales of fancy.

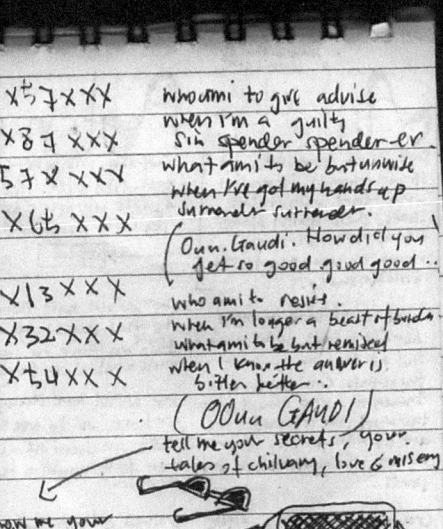

There's a void in my being.
A subtle feeling — It starts from my bones
of falling out, falling short of
that i'm falling short, falling out

i'm afraid that   Will you wait,
surrounded by opinions. I'll watch you
                         Empire fall.
I'm lost in the deep end.
which thoughts are my own? x2
┌─────────────────────────────────┐
│ Nothing is certain but expanse │
└─────────────────────────────────┘
          ↓
which ones I condone.

WRAP ME UP IN CLOTH.
SHEETS OF THAT WITH
         YOUR SCENT LINGERS

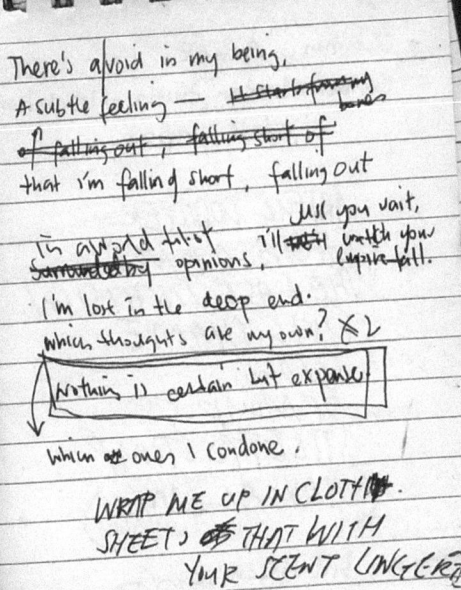

bones & it flows into my arteries, arteries / And there, I let it
linger till it's a cancer in me, a cancer in me.
I'm falling short, I'm falling out of love.
There's a world of opinions! Attempting incisions / Attempt through
to my chest to arrest the breath in my lungs, breath of my lungs.
I'm falling short, I'm falling out of love.
Someday, I'll be the girl of your dreams, but not, for now.
Someday, you'll understand the unforeseen but not within me.
There's a burning fire / doomed to expire / It started from a flame & it blazes
out of my ribs, out of my ribs / And there my heart lays trapped in its cage.
trapped in its cage.
There's a form in my head / A vice locked in its gain / The gulf lies
in my veins & narrates the death of my soul, of my soul.
I'm falling short, I'm falling out of love.

The last INCISION.

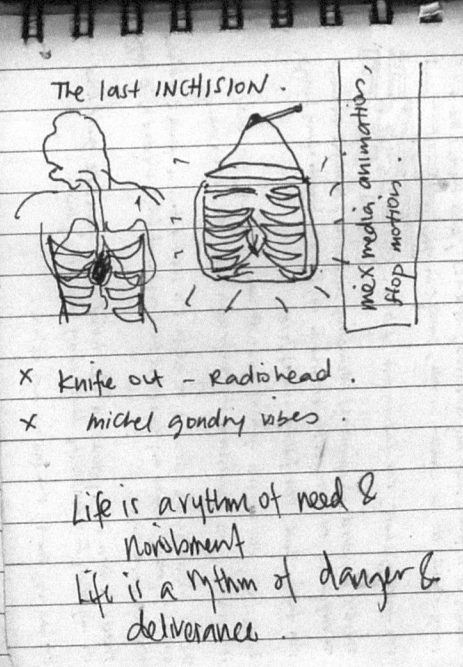

mix media, animation,
stop motion

x knife out — Radiohead.
x michel gondry vibes.

Life is a rythm of need &
nourishment
Life is a rythm of danger &
deliverance

THE CHEFALO KNOT

you're a little old to be chasing young skirts out of
boredom. your youth was once a gift but it failed to be
translated into wisdom.
Well maybe in another universe where age is just a number.
But woe is thee, as your curiosity is up against gravity.

you're a little sick in the head to luff at lambs like its
all casual. your charm may be convincing but it's not
like it was ever really factual.
well maybe, in another universe where a monogamist is
a sinner. But woe is thee, as your curiosity is up
against gravity.

It would be wise, It would be wise, it would be wise.
to stop flirting with me.

you're a little intese but i don't take any offense of
your advancements. flattery it may be but its perversity
out weights all my judgement.
well maybe, in another universe where age is just a
number. But woe is thee, as your curiosity is
up against gravity.

---

album song l
gaudi
dear param
chefalo kno
civil shame
artful dodg
inch asim
gbw
lyre lyre he
some kind
armours
stiletto stom
conscience
quit you.

YOUR THE ARTFUL DODGER. THE
CLASSIC DANGER & I'M ASHAMED
OF MYSELF. CAUSE THIS IS ALL TOO
FAMILIAR. OH HOW COULD I HAVE
JUMPED INTO THE COLD WITH THE
UNPREDICTABLE. THE REST IS PREDIC-
TABLE. HOW COULD I HAVE JUMPED
INTO BED, WITH THE FRIVOLOUS. WHY
DID I HAVE TO CHALLENGE THE
UNIVERSE. YOU'RE THE ARTFUL
DODGER, MY HEARTBEAT STOPPER &
YOU'RE HIDING BEHIND YOUR WALL
OF HUMOUR. **THE ARTFUL DODGER**

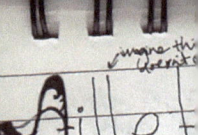

imagine th
doesn't

Stillet

She's gonna stomp (sto
stomp (stomp), stom
your heart with stil
shoes. she's gonna s
(stomp), stomp (stom
stomp on your hea
stiletto shoes.

who would have th
her black hole of
will be consuming
thoughts, consum
thoughts. who w
thought, she'd m
art of dismantlin
heart, disassem
parts.

Crowned a victo
victim she plays
a skin with bea
plagues. Born
vicious she sta
prey writhins
floor. you're

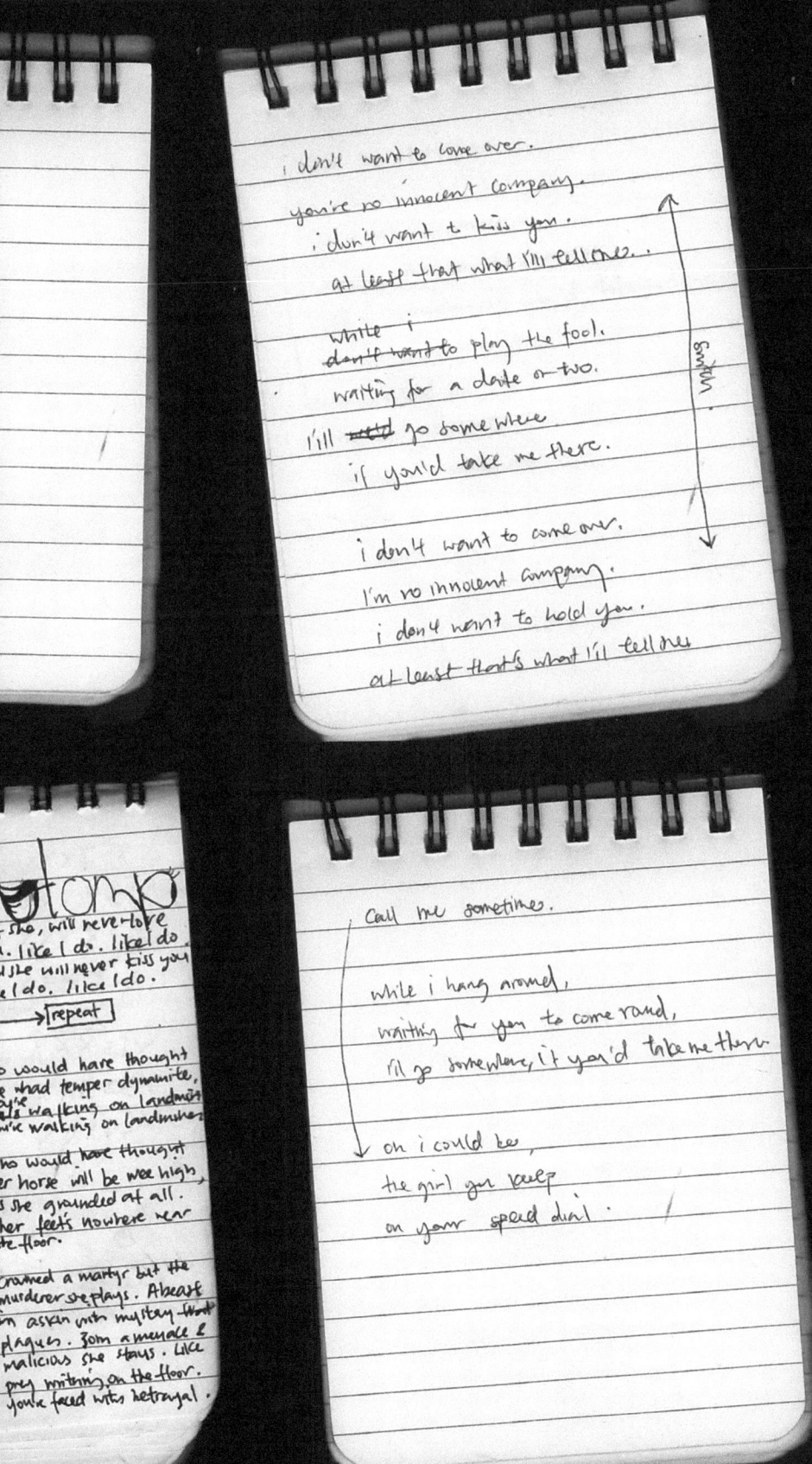

(sketch: lasalle blackbox stage with labels: loadin, lights, curtains, entrance)

lasalle blackbox

Total DI → 3 × DI Box
Mic stands → 10 × stands
guitar mics → 2 × mics
XLR cables → 15 (super super long)

score kwek on lights
(check what needs to be done)
NAC provides:
- scaffolding (hang shirt)

XXIII stage layout.

(stage layout sketch with labels: guitar, guitar, bass DI, 1 kick, 1 snare, 2 overhead, 6 on 2 out)

Backline:

① drum kit ⎫
  - kick
  - ~~dr~~ snare   ⎬ Thunder rock
  - floor tom
  - tom   ⎭
  - cymbals
  - carpet   → leonard's studio
② bass amp   → deon's
③ guitar amp (AC30 copy)
④ guitar amp (night train)
⑤ keyboards → esther
⑥ extra floor tom →
⑦ Acoustic guitar →
⑧ main vocals → SM5
⑨ backup vocals

tuesday, december 13, 2011

drowning.

The's just so much to do. So little time. So ~~much~~ much to plan ahead for and so much uncertainty. So much that i feel but no capacity for either. I'm drowning in feelings and drowning in work. ~~good work but it's not like it doesn't come with it's stresses~~. It's good work I shouldn't complain.

I'm just feeling alot of pressure. I don't want to disappoint him. and I'm ~~guilty~~ feeling guilty that i have to. I can't be what you want me to be. I'm not what you think i am. i just feel so... insufficient in all areas of my life. ~~like I'm already a let down before I even~~ inch, just get over it. teach yourself how to swim in bullshit or drown.

Gaudi

Who am i to give advise
when i'm a guilty sin
spender spender-er
What am i to be but wise
when i've got my hands up
surrender surrender.

Ouuuu Gaudi,
how did you get so good
at being cool.

Who am i to resist
when i'm no longer a beast of
burden burden.
What am i to be but remiss
when i know the answer is
bitter bitter.

Ouuuu Gaudi,
how did you get so good
at being cool.

so tell me your secrets
your tales of chivalry, love & misery
oh show me your daggers
the fate you fancy, obey & bury
oh tell me, oh tell me

EATING THE CRUST OF HUMILITY.

i never liked the edges of a bread.
i'd always cut em off. always.

but then i stopped.

partly cause i felt wasteful
but mostly because
i picked convenience over desire.

but until one day,
i was served a sangwich with no edges.

i had it
and i loved it.

and spent the rest of the meal
staring at my open faced sangwich,
wonder why i never pursued my breads
to have no edges anymore
and the only reason i could conjure was
stupid.

i just simply... forgot.

but nevermore.

By the wear of my face,
i shall eat edgeless bread,
till i return to the ground.

No matter the circumstance,
i'm choosing to be cutting edge.

THINGS TO SURF

1. ~~Joseph & the elevenstars~~
2. ~~devil, reb & satan~~
3. most expensive painting in the world
4. ~~Nepal / Cambodia (backpacking)~~
5. ~~_____~~
6. ~~woody Allen - Annie Hall~~
7. woody Allen - Manhattan
8. ~~Harmony Korine~~
9. ~~Maps & Atlas - Perch Patchwork~~
10. ~~Elliott Smith - Figure 8~~
11. Marvin's Room - Jerry Zaks
12. ~~Alan Parsons Project~~
13. I wanna hold your hand - Bob Zemeckis
14. the frighteners - Peter Jackson
15. **The devil & daniel johnston**
16. the wire man (documentary)
17. cultural deserts (context: sci)
18. ~~artist like license~~
19. around glasses.
20.

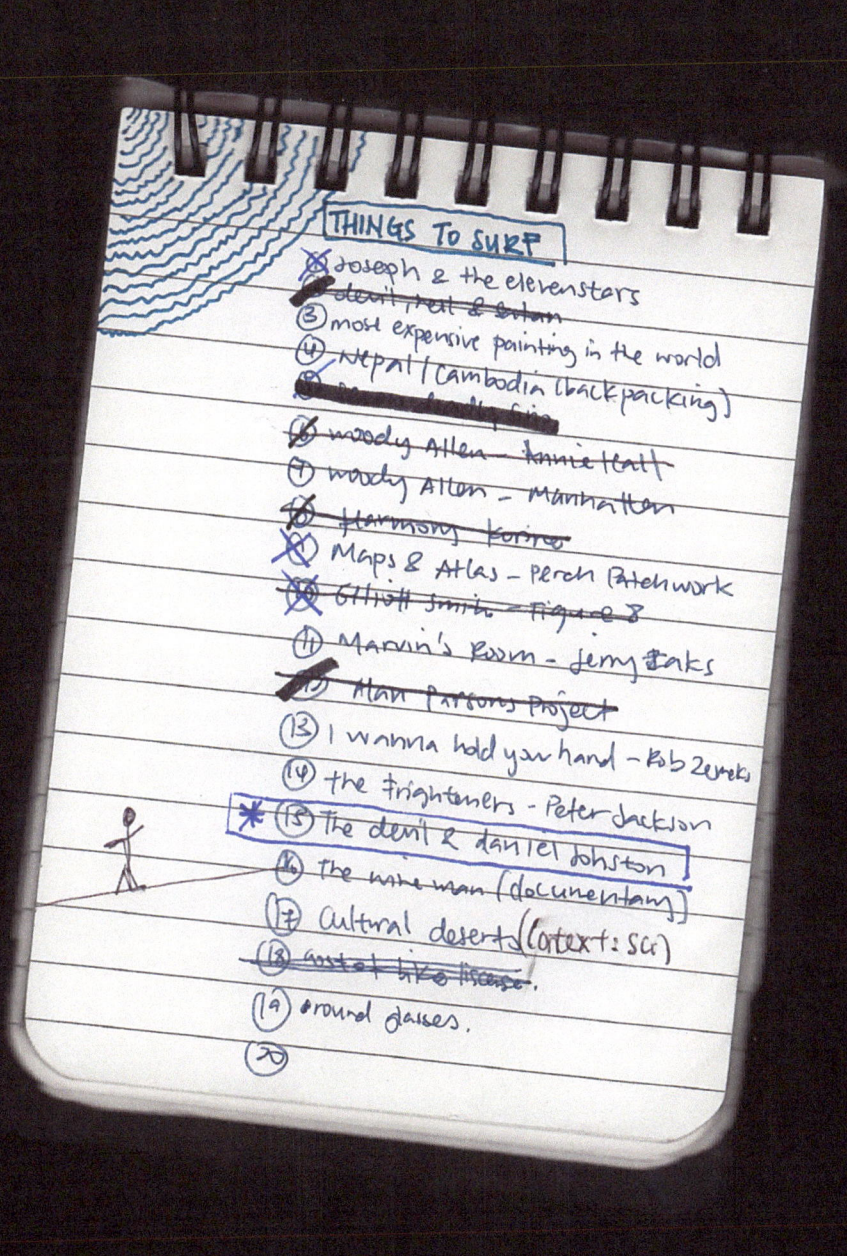

can't
~~cannot~~

i ~~can't~~ quit you,
i can't do without
I can't quit you

To quit you. I (
I can't quit you

I can't do with out my
I can't follow anyone
I can't core you o(

```
        2x212x
        4x45xx
2x212x  7x767x
4x45xx  9x9(10)xx
9x989x
9x9(10)xx → 8x89xx
                7x78xx
```

right down to the bone!

I'm remi(
freedom

~~x4~~ x5465x
5x465x
355433
688766
vice
knows I've tried... 577655

vacate you out of my mind.
system override

x7687x
5x665x
my spine. 8 ⑩ ⑩ 98x / 77987x
        hollow
heart's turned ~~empty~~ (heart/brains/
the burrows of my ~~body~~   body)

a in all of the things we
have in common.
n gasping for air —
the same air we share

              I'm
of how ~~your~~ faithful to my
ow you're spineless with your feelings

lonely hearts on i

Written by Evelyn Choo.

We're on a voyage to no where,
    sailing away from the trouble land.
    abandoning those hearts on fire,
   hold on tight we're nearly half way there.

brushes with the death of us
    can only make us more beautiful
    but if it kills with no mercy
  just know that i loved you with all my heart.

don't you think we've gone too far
    stealing the sunset from everyone
    its funny how it seems so right
      stealing the sunset from everyone.

if i had a time machine,
    will you jump on board
    we'll go back to one
    it stabs my heart but this i'll say
    you're the only one i'll open my eyes to.

you're the only one i'll open my eyes to.

"Do you know that indium (IN) is a very soft, silvery-white metal with a brilliant lustre and it gives a high-pitched "scream" when bent. and CH4 is a molecular compound called methane which has clean burning qualities that makes for excellent fuel.

if you combined indium and methane, you'd get INCH4. or a hot singer"

– **Leonard Soosay**

Tuesday, May 22, 2012.

God makes no mistakes. I'm pretty aware of that. but i can't seem to stop questioning myself on a daily basis. Everything I do and I'm about to do feels like a mistake. Its like playing chess with the computer. - one bad move - you're set. The 'game over' is already pre-determined but you'd still have to play through the whole game, just to find out you can't win at the end. Seriously, what the hell am i doing with myself? my self-worth has been on this spiralling descent. i should just take comfort that God makes no mistakes. And no matter what pre-destined mistakes I have, I should just stay honest with myself to find the takeaways. ok.

I'm glad i broke up with ███████ 'cause I'm actually seeing him dig deeper than before. ever since my departure. sounds harsh, but I can see that the relationship we had

Thursday, May 22, 2012

was such a distraction for both of us. But if God makes no mistakes, I guess it means that it happened for a reason, continued for a reason... and now that it's over, it has ended for a reason.

We've been chewing each other out in circles. I've made him feel like crap about himself. which has in turn point the finger at me — makes me feel like like a crappy human being. dammit. I don't know if I can be or am who he wants or needs me to be for him. well lets not sugar coat it inch, you're not. you've failed. evidently. i guess you are what uncle ▓ says you are.

lovers should inspire each other, friends should enrich each other. I should be reminding him about something he's forgotten about himself. Instead, we're both become mirrors of our shortcomings.

The truth is, ███████ was <u>never</u> mine to begin with. it's been a hard pill to swallow.

I'm so proud of who he is today. literally no thanks to me. i always knew he was meant for great things, I guess i just never figured that God would exclude me from those things.

dear God, i pray for grace as i try my best to be obedient to your word. I pray for the instincts to lean on you. Thank you for your mercy and love through the people around me. Help me cut the chords of this chapter of my life. Help me cut the chord, burn the rope & bury the crater deep.

Wednesday, August 8, 2012

Being an honest actor is tough. I guess it depends of the philosophy you choose to adopt. The philosophy needs to be compatible with one personality. I'm being too sensitive, so much that it really gets to me, and I'm not really functioning well cause I'm affected. Is it a goo... thing. Besides displaying real portrayal, is being a good actor mean that I have to be good at compartmentalizing myself? Or is this an all or nothing business? Or convincingly taking the shit out of my own emotions? Where do i find the "pleasure" in playing a charate of pain? food for thou...

Old Nine

Oh you're,
the first and maybe the last
A major minor memory,
here to haunt my stage.

and i'm the fool of all fools.
i jumped into the deep without my clothes again.

oh you're the first and maybe the last.
a summer i know that won't repeat itself.
a lover from a scene that i can't dispel.

a subtle pleasantry.
a puppet that i can't grasp.

oh, excuse me mister.
won't you repeat the question.
cause i sure hope that i could be the answer.

oh, excuse me mister.
won't you repeat the question.
cause i sure hope that i could be the answer.

to all that your heart desires and all the your flesh requires.

oh you're the first and maybe the last.
you can break my heart a thousand times over,
the theatre won't mind cause that's what the script told you.

a bitter pleasantry. i'll be the puppet that you once, fancied.

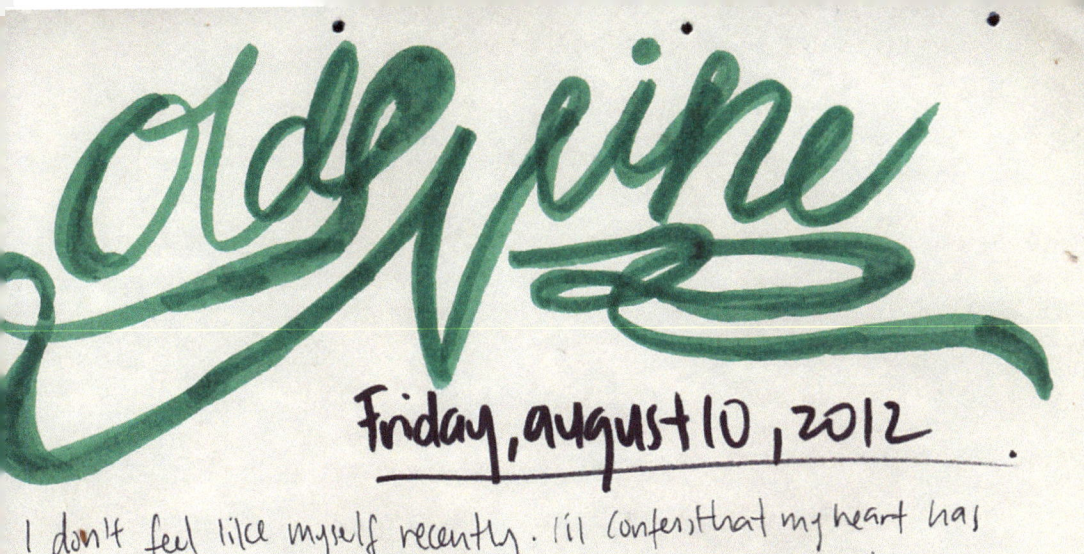

Friday, August 10, 2012

I don't feel like myself recently. I'll confess that my heart has been feeling ridiculously heavy. But I've been burying my feelings instead of confronting them with work. which isn't really out of the norm. It's just kind of ironic that the work that I'm doing these days requires me to confront my emotions. Urgh. This stupid shit clock of mine I call a heart is just so bloody messy. Being busy seems to be the only solution to cope. Blewghhh... The musical has been great. Got totally schooled by jianhong. It's awesome and all but I believe the floodgates are open, and I just don't. Urgh. don't know how to compute all this... feelings. I've been taking они home with me every night & crying my eyeballs out. don't get me wrong, I'm really grateful for all that 老师 has done for me but, thanks to doing 老师 - I've unknowingly knowingly allowed a meteor to puncture a gapping hole to my emotional defenses. Lo & BEHOLD! A huge crater in my heart.

▇▇▇▇ is not moving on. I have no idea how to cope. and balance being platonic friends, best friends or ex-lovers. I'm utter guiltstriken and it's hard to be kind for I fear it would be mistaken. I don't want to be the asshole to mislead. Argghhh. God, if this is a test. I CAN HANDLE IT! KEEP ME STEADY. Heal my

xx8658
xx5656

```
         Ab7         Cm7         F7
   Ab
  |G#    |G#5/7      |Cm7b5      |F7         |
                  2
    Bbm    Cm         Bm            Eb7
  |D#m7   |Cm        |Bm         |D#9        |


                          Bbm
  |       |          |B♭7  B7    Eb7
  |       |Cm        |B♭7        |D#9        |


    Dbm     Dbm      Dbm        Dbm
  |C#m    |C#m      |C#m        |C#m         |
    Bbm     Bbm       Eb7         Cb7
  |B♭m    |B♭m      |D#9        |D#9         |


  |A#2/7  |Dm7b5    |G#^7       |G#6         |

  |G#7    |         |          |            |
```

CHORUS:

|A#²/₇ B♭m |A#²/₇ |~~C#△7~~ Dm7♭5 Bm7 D7 |Dm7♭5 |

|C#△7 ~~B♭m~~ |C#△7 |G#6 A♭ |G#7 A♭7 |

|A#m9 B♭m |A#m9 |C7 C7 |C7 |

end A♭

Bumfuzzle

> **bum·fuz·zle** [buhm-fuhz-*uh*l]
> *verb (used with object),* bum·fuz·zled,
> bum·fuz·zling.
> to <u>confuse</u> or <u>fluster</u>.
>
> **origin:**
> 1900–05; *bum-* (expressive prefix, perhaps to be
> identified with the initial syllable of <u>bamboozle</u>)
> + *fuzzle* to confuse (perhaps expressive alteration
> of <u>fuddle</u>)

His heart's black
and hollow,
He changes the
colours of his eyes
as he please.
Oh his words
trigger havoc.
His humanity's
intact but it's
left diseased.

His face is cold and somber
But he rages inside
with the vengeance
of beasts.
Oh even when he's sober,
a bloody nose is what he'll have you receive.

The vagrant lover is loyal to heartache,
lost between the flustered heart &
confused head.
Forever responsible for the love I've tamed,
one can only attempt to...
cut the chord, burn the rope
& bury the corpse deep.

Oh he choked to death a dozen times
for swallowing his pride. oh no
mercy from the mercenary,
while the world bears the brunt of his blade.

Wednesday, August 22, 2012

We're almost half way through recording the new record now. Drums are all tracked, bass is all tracked, most guitars are tracked. Just left with some vocal tracking and a crap load of backups left to do. Need to start fixing the girls' schedule. Urghh. But I'm starting to get into the phase where everything sounds like shit to me.

Anyways, while ~~having~~ having some teh today at the kopitiam below Leonard's, it just dawned on me that ▬▬ was the starting point that sparked off my bumpuzzle journey. Complications have always been a staple for ~~me~~ me. I don't have a better explanation other than the fact that I've always been so damn loyal to heartache.

Part of me wants to thank him for evoking the skill of cutting chords, burning ropes and burying craters, out of me. NOT saying I'm an expert at it because... I still struggle — evidently.

> m loyal to heartache.
> I'm a
> vagabond / muse
> vagrant / traveller
> priviledged peddler.

> respects a currency you can't afford! / a privilege peddler ought to know his flaws — but he said Perfect love cost everything

Bumfuzzle tuning

Tuning

D#
G#
C#
~~F#~~
G
D#

Pre Chorus

xx 9 7 8 0
xx 11 12 11 0
xx 9 7 8 0
~~xx 11 12 11 0~~

xx 8 7 8 0

xx 5 4 5 0

7 5 # 4

x 5 x x 6 x
x 7 x x 5 7
x 9 x x 10
x 10 x x 11

Tuning is same

CHORUS

x	10	10	0	8	0	B
x	5	5	0	3	0	F#
x	3	3	0	1	0	E
x	12	12	0	9	0	C#m
x	14	14	0	11	0	D#m
x	14	14	13	12	0	D# Maj

B

Standard tuning - 1st/1 cape

↓   ↑   ↓ ↑
F   F#   F#   C# G# A   A   C#
(2nd string)(1 snd string)(2nd string)(2nd string)(2)(1)(2)(7x7)
 8 fret   2nd fret 9th fret -4th   x   x   x
                                       11f   C   12

Fm   x8x89x
C#M7   x4654x
F#M7   2x332x
A#m   6x66xx
B7   7x778xx

Verse - standard tuning

Bm   F#   ~~B#~~ D#1/2dimish / E#m7 flat5
                   x6767x

~~Bm~~   C#M   F#M   D#1/2dimish

Bbm
                              C 1/2dim
Bbm   C#M   C#1/2dim   x3434x
             x4545x

→ white ~~cork~~ CD hubs.

INCH.CHUA
BUMFUZZLE

N S
↓
— magnetic closures

→ cut holes. through to see CD.
× magnetic CD jackets
↓
extra heavy laminated board.
× pop up CD cover.
× Black fiber board.

CD tray options
- fibre board tray.
- cork hub tray
- blank digipak (white)
- white hub adhesive

stitched
→ book binder style

6-p insert.

→ hub

× vertical
× landscape

Notebook style (Horizontal)

stitching

Things to include
1 × CD
1 × strip of tape
1 × insert.

"loyal"
"A vagrant lover ~~is loyal to misters~~, A raging fire ~~cut the chord~~, is loyal to confusion. burn the ropes..."

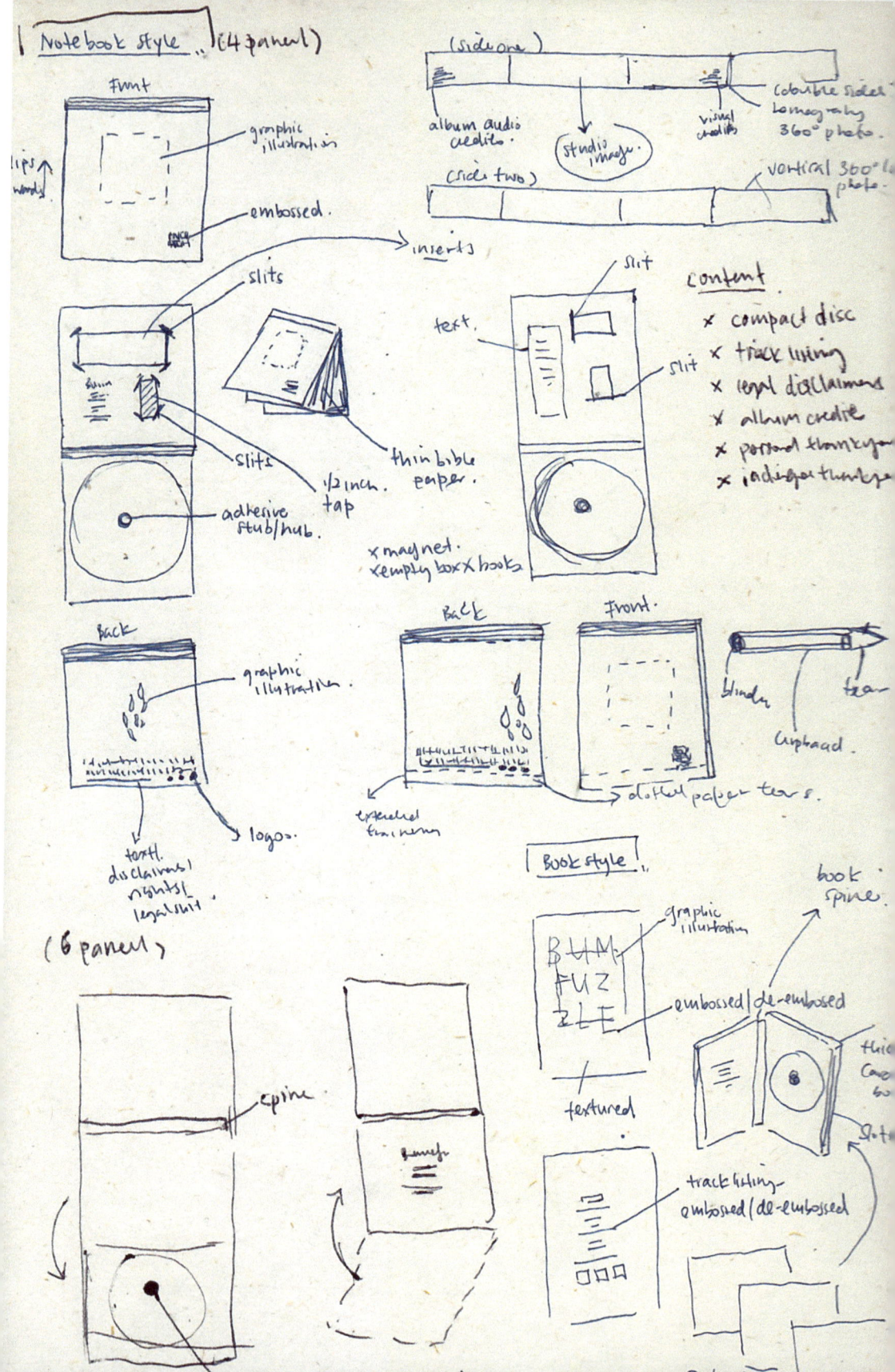

Production Progress.

No.	Songs	Duration	BPM	Inch Chua					Mark John	Patrick Taylor			Dalton Sim	Beni/Mel
				Vox	Bckg Vox	Gtr	O-chrd/Synth		E Gtr	Upright	E Bass	Percussions	Drums	Backup Vox
1	Gaudi	3:39	91	x	x	x			x		x		x	x
2	The Chefalo Knot	3:44	127	x	x	x			x		x	x	x	x
3	Quit You	3:03	125	x	x	x			x		x	x	x	x
4	Artful Dodger	2:51	87	x	x	x			x		x		x	x
5	Lyre Lyre Hearts On Fire	3:23	119	x	x	x			x	x			x	x
6	Inchcision	5:00	125	x	x	x			x		x	x	x	x
7	Old Nine	2:50	139	x	x	x	x		x		x	x	x	x
8	Dear Paramour	4:51	93/133	x		x			x	x	x	x	x	x
9	Bumfuzzle (Go up in smokes)	3:34	170	x	x	x			x		x	x	x	x (?)
10	Glow	4:29	67	x	x	x			x	x	x	x		
	Pending Songs													
11	Armours	4:03	117/93				x		x		x		x	
12	Shame Stain Of The Civil Slave / Civil Shame	3:25	113			x			x		x		x	
13	Stiletto Stomp	2:57	125						x		x		x	

deep blue sea. (Folksong)

deep blue sea, honey, deep deep blue sea.
deep blue sea, honey, deep deep blue sea.
it was me, who walked up drowned out in the
deep blue sea.

dig my grave with a silver, silver spade
dig my grave with a silver, sivers spade.
it was me, who walked up drowned out in the
deep blue sea.

wrap me up, with a silken, silken shroud
wrap me up, with a silken, sikens shroud.
it was me, who walked up drowned out in the
deep blue sea

golden sun, bring me back, bring me back
golden sun, bring me back, bring me back
it was me, who walked up drowned out in the
deep blue sea.

deep blue sea, honey, deep deep blue sea.
deep blue sea, honey, deep deep blue sea.

Friday, Feb 22, 2013

Just left Manila, crossing the pacific ocean for the umpteenth time with Pete Seeger keeping me company. i love, love, love, ~~for~~ crossing the pacific ocean. i'm always reminded of the magnitude of my ambitions as the plane glides over the largest of the earth's oceanic devisions.

plane rides over the sea are like savepoints/checkpoints if my life was a video game.

I'm a different person each time i cross the deep blue sea. And it's funny how i only realize it and mull over my change while i cross the ocean.

There's a pleasant isolation that happens in the middle of the ocean: a point where one's presence precedes presence. It's as if a part of me and

Monday, Feb 25, 2013

My existence boards a metal bird that takes me to purgatory... the deep blue sea.

There's something about being in between places — one naturally ponders on what lies ahead, what is left behind, who you were before, who you are now, and who you will need to be.

ABOUT THE AUTHOR

Inch Chua is a native Singaporean musician, artist, and writer currently residing in New York City, NY. Chua has produced two full length albums, and her accomplishments have prized her with features in Cosmopolitan, Nylon, Esquire, and The Wall Street Journal. Chua has spoken on platforms such as TEDxWomen, Social Media Week, Singapore Music Society and has played numerous music festivals across the world such as, South by Southwest (Austin, Texas), MIDI Music Festival (Beijing, China), World Expo (Shanghai, China), Canadian Music Festival (Toronto, Canada), Music Matters (Singapore) and Baybeats (Singapore). Between The Devil & The Deep Blue Sea is Chua's first book.

ABOUT THE ALTAR COLLECTIVE

The Altar Collective is a small press located in Los Angeles. Their titles have received recognition from publications like Dog Dance Diary and LADYGUNN, and have been picked up by notable outlets, such as designer Marc Jacobs' bookstore, Bookmarc. Chua's book, "Between The Devil & The Deep Blue Sea" is the first of The Altar Collective's Orchard Series, which gives readers a unique opportunity to get to know a musician through their book.

www.ingramcontent.com/pod-product-compliance
Lightning Source LLC
Chambersburg PA
CBHW042058290426
44113CB00001B/9